A CANTERBURY GIRL

ISBN 0 9524094 1 0
Tritton Publications
2 Salts Avenue Loose
Maidstone Kent ME15 OAY

First published October 1998
Printed by E.C. Parker & Company (Services) Ltd Canterbury Kent

British Library Cataloguing in Publication Data
A catalogue record for this book is available from the British Library

A Canterbury Girl

Memories and pictures
of life in a cathedral city

Mary Tritton

Contents

Author's acknowledgements

My thanks to Ellen Fuller (née Jones) and Ted Scoones for their contributions to Chapters 2 and 7 respectively, and to the following friends and relatives who lent photographs, supplied information or helped me in other ways while I was compiling this book: Phyllis Browne (née Gibbs), Derek Butler, Evelyn Child (née Easton), Peter Cole, Sally Coleman (née Phillips), 'Bobbie' Davis (née Goulden), Elsie Eden (née Theoff), Evelyn Goddard (née Bowen), Margaret Goodban (née Nicholls), Harry Nicholls, Nita Rigden (née Baker), Howard Smith, Kathleen Steddy (née Kennett), Nigel Tilly, Christopher Tritton, Norah Tritton (née Child), Pat Tritton (née Sackett), Joan Wallis, Alan Walton, Joyce Walton (née Savery); and Paul Tritton, my editor and publisher.

Main cover picture: *The Westgate Towers and F. H. Nicholls' shop at No. 7 St Dunstan's Street, from a watercolour by Sidney J. ('Toby') Nash, December 1933.*

The picture on the wall

I bought the picture postcard reproduced below at a collectors' fair at the Westgate Hall (formerly the Territorial Army Drill Hall) in St Peter's Lane. It is the same view as my 'picture on the wall' and was published by H.J. Goulden Limited of Canterbury. Despite the ink smudges it gives a very good impression of St Dunstan's Street as I knew it when I was a child.

ABOUT ten years ago I went into a building society on the corner of Dover Street, Canterbury, and as I opened the door I saw, on the wall opposite me, a large photograph of St Dunstan's Street and the Westgate Towers. A little girl could be seen about to enter the side door of the baker's and pastrycook's shop next door to the *Falstaff Hotel*. I knew at once that that little girl was me. It was as if time had stood still; a snapshot of history, with me in it!

I bought a huge enlargement of the photograph for my dining room wall. As I look at it today, many things come to mind .

The picture was taken in 1921, when I was eight years old. I suppose that, in those days, the photographer would have set up his camera on a tripod and taken a time exposure — but perhaps not, because some of the people are on the move, yet are not blurred.

The *Falstaff Hotel* has changed since those days, but not much; unfortunately the portrait of Falstaff on the sign on the wrought iron bracket is not visible in the photograph. Perhaps the portrait had faded, or could not be seen because the photograph was taken against the light.

The baker's shop belonged to my father, Frederick Nicholls, and I can see the sunblinds which he would have pulled down earlier in the day. I notice too that my mother, Alice, has opened

one of the bedroom windows. In my mind's eye I can see Dad coming out of the side door, pushing his barrow.

A very elegant lady is walking along the pavement on the left of the picture. Further along a Simon Langton schoolgirl, wearing the panama hat and coat which was the school's uniform at that time, is pushing her bicycle towards the Westgate Towers. She is passing Nash & Co., the tailors, and Miss Welsh's shop on the corner of North Lane.

Further on, near the lamp post, two ladies are having a chat beside an ice-cream barrow. We knew one of them as 'the old Italian'. She came into our shop frequently, for her bread, and was a member of either the Coia or the Salvatori family. Coai's ice-cream was well known and very popular in the 1920s.

A 'horse bus' that belonged to one of the hotels — probably the *County* — is approaching the towers; it has been to Canterbury West railway station, to pick up some visitors.

The lady crossing the road seems about to be knocked down by the oncoming car, which can be seen round the corner. A trade van is also approaching and is rather too close for comfort to the man on the bicycle.

The buildings on the right are Mr H. Hatton's restaurant on the corner of Westgate Grove; Edward Wood's grocery shop at No. 93; 'The Gun' Dining Rooms, run by Herbert Skelton; William Penney's fish shop at No. 91; W. & R. Fletcher's butcher's shop; Mr F.R. Arnold's St Dunstan's Floral Nursery shop at No. 89; and Sidney Terry's electrical shop (under the bay window). Just visible

This photograph was taken in the summer of 1996. My daughter-in-law, Patricia, is playing the part of the elegant lady of the early 1920s seen in the previous picture, and has just passed the *Bishop's Finger* pub, which was called the *George and Dragon* when I was a girl. I am waiting for Pat where, 75 years earlier, I was photographed entering the side door to my father's bakery, which is now a betting shop.

The Westgate Towers, Canterbury, viewed from the street outside the house where I was born 85 years ago. This drawing by William Bartlett was published in 1828 – 85 years before I was born. Children, traders and dogs throng the street and among the fascinating details are a small boy and a monkey, seen at the corner of North Lane being sent on their way by a city official.

next door to Mr Terry is the tradesmen's entrance to Westgate House, owned by the Misses Laurie; the stone ball on the wall beside the entrance is still there today.

The shadows tell me that the photograph was taken in the early afternoon.

I only wish that my parents could see my 'picture on the wall.' It is a very treasured possession and I shall pass it on to my family; it was one of my inspirations and an aide-memoir during the past few years, while I wrote this volume of memories of my life as 'a Canterbury girl.'

I have not done this for personal gain or fame, but to recall memories of my generation and give some pleasure, especially to my school friends and to my workmates at Gouldens, the shop in Canterbury High Street where I worked from the time I left school until I was married.

Sadly many of my old friends have passed on, but I remember them with great affection.

I hope the present generation will also enjoy reading about the 1920s and 30s — such as what it was like at school (where discipline was strict, but where we were happy and respected our teachers); and what it was like to go shopping, when the customers were 'always right' and there were chairs for them to sit on while they chose their purchases and arranged to have them delivered at any time, anywhere.

My story begins in 1913, the year I was born, and although mainly concerned with everyday life in the city 'between the wars' I have included some of my memories of the Second World War and later years.

I finished writing this book as I approached my 85th birthday, realising that I have many happy times to look back on; and much to be thankful for.

'When this book you see,
remember me;
And bear me in your
mind.
Let all the world say what
they will;
Speak of me as you find.'
ANON

1: An Edwardian marriage

The picture below epitomizes the golden summers and elegance of the Edwardian age. It was taken on June 17, 1907 after the wedding at Godalming, Surrey, of my parents Frederick Holness Nicholls (standing third left) and Emily Alice Calver (seated third left). With them are: (back row) George Calver, Lena Nicholls, Emma Calver, William Smith, Alice Calver and Harry Calver; (front row) May Calver, Bert Calver, Kate Calver, Fanny Calver, 'Queenie' (a foster child), Emily Mary Calver (the bride's mother) and Lilian Calver.

MY mother, Emily Alice Calver (always known as Alice), was born in Eastbourne on March 18, 1880. She was one of four daughters of George Calver and Emily Mary Calver (née Stokes); their other daughters were Emma, Fanny and Kate and they also had two sons, George and Harry.

Some time after my mother was born the family moved to Godalming, Surrey, where Grandfather Calver worked as a tailor. He made clothes for Charter House School and Mum told me that he sat cross-legged on a table to sew, as tailors did in those days. He died in December 1902, aged only 51 years; Grandmother Calver died in the 1930s.

My father, Frederick Holness Nicholls, was born on May 2, 1878. At one time his father, Thomas, lived at Harbledown, Canterbury, where I believe he worked as a coachman at Hall Place for Mr Cox of Cox & Scott, wholesale grocers, of No. 42 Station Road West, Canterbury.

Earlier, Thomas had been a coachman at Hales Place, St Stephen's, where I believe my father was born. Thomas was a soldier in the Crimean war and served with the Royal Horse Artillery — the 'Galloping Gunners.' He died in August 1906 and his grave is in Brookwood Cemetery, Surrey.

For the last eight years of his life he was a Chelsea Pensioner and I treasure a photograph showing him in his scarlet uniform and tricorn hat, wearing his Crimea Medal 1854 - 1865 and clasps,

At Warren Farm, New Romney, c. 1902. My maternal grandmother Emily Mary Calver (née Stokes), is third from the left; with her are Jane (née Stokes) Austen, John Austen, Fanny Austen and Fanny Calver (Emily's daughter).

Turkish Crimea Medal 1854 - 1856 and Long Service and Good Conduct Medal 1855 - 1874. The picture was taken by G. Thomson, whose studio was at No.70 Northgate, Canterbury, opposite Broad Street.

I know very little about my paternal grandmother, Emily Nicholls (née Baker). She was born in Blean in about 1847. Thomas Nicholls was her second husband. My parents told me that her first husband was a member of the Baker family of Canterbury hoteliers and that by him she had two children, Alfred and Percy. Thomas and Emily had three daughters, Eva, Ethel and Lena, and two sons, Hope and Frederick. Hope Nicholls had a greengrocery shop at No. 27 St Dunstan's, next to the railway crossing.

I am not sure where my parents first met but in his youth my father worked for a baker by the name of Daniels, whose shop was in the High Street at New Romney. Dad delivered bread to Iden Parsonage, where Mum was in service as a parlour maid to the Reverend and Mrs Bates; he was the Vicar of Iden, near Rye.

Mum told me all about her days at the Parsonage, where the Bates' entertained a lot: in those days the parson was virtually the local squire. Coutts the bankers stayed there as did, among others, the Forbes Robertsons, the well-known theatrical family. They all used to have archery contests on the Parsonage lawns.

My mother was related to the Carey and Austen families, who lived on Romney Marsh. Her cousin Fanny married David Carey. In her younger days Mum made many visits to her Uncle John and Aunt Jane Austen at Warren Farm, New Romney.

I once had a holiday at Pear Tree House, in New Romney High Street, with my Aunt Fanny Carey. There are still Careys on the Marsh, and I remember that at one time there was a firm called Carey's Coaches.

In 1907 Alfred Baker helped Dad buy a bakery and pastry-cook's shop at No. 7 St Dunstan's Street and this became my parents' home and business for the next 29 years.

My paternal grandparents Thomas and Emily Nicholls, pictured sometime in the 1880s by H.B. Collis of Canterbury. Thomas proudly displays the medals he won while serving with the Royal Horse Artillery. Opposite page: Thomas as a Chelsea Pensioner.

G. Thompson

70 NORTHGATE
CANTERBURY.

11

My maternal grandparents, George and Emily Calver. Below: my parents, Fred and Alice Nicholls, photographed at Stringers Studio, No. 11 Station Road West, Canterbury.

Members of the Canterbury and District Master Bakers' Association on the float they built for the Canterbury Carnival Procession in August, 1909. Left to right: (1) Fred Nicholls, (2) an unidentified baker, (3) possibly G. H. Coe, pastrycook, of No. 2 The Borough, (4) G. Saunders, baker and confectioner of No. 50 St Peter's Street, (5) Alfred Webb. The float features a windmill, sacks of flour and examples of the bakers' decorative skills, and bids success to Kent's cricketers in their forthcoming match against Australia. The result was a draw: Kent 319 all out, Australia 522 for 9. A few minutes after this picture was taken, disaster struck and the float had to withdraw from the procession. My mother, who owned the photograph, told me that the reason for this was that when the time came to tow the float from the yard where it was built, it was found to be too wide to pass through the gates! However, one of the baker's daughters told me that the float collapsed as soon as someone climbed inside the windmill to rotate the sails. According to a report in the *Kentish Gazette* the float was wrecked in London Road when its horses were startled by a torchbearer and bolted. The float made a successful appearance in the 1910 carnival, winning first prize for the best trade entry.

The picture above, from a Gouldens postcard, depicts the Westgate end of St Dunstan's a few years before my parents took over the bakery at No. 7, next door to the *Falstaff Hotel*. The name of the previous owner, Mr Whittaker, can be seen below the first floor windows. A milkman is on his rounds, with the big brass churn from which he filled the jugs that his customers brought to their doors. A lady with a perambulator is looking at the goods displayed in Mr Whittaker's window and one of the ladies standing nearby is wearing a straw boater – very fashionable in Edwardian times. Among the premises seen opposite No. 7 are the *Gun Tavern* (which later became the Gun Dining Rooms) at No. 92 and, at No. 91, a toy shop owned by a Mr H. Nicholls. When I was a girl William Penney, fishmonger, took over the shop.

Members of the Canterbury and District Master Bakers' Association, pictured a year or two after their carnival debacle. Members identified are (from the left) second row from front: (1) Fred Nicholls, (4) Alfred Webb, (5) Ernest T. Newing (chairman) of No. 9 Upper Bridge Street, (8) H.M. Swain of No. 42 Stour Street; third row: (1) G. Saunders of No. 50 St Peter's Street, (2) F.W. Finnis of 13 Butchery Lane; back row: (1) E. Hopper of No. 80 Wincheap Street, (2) A.E. Gaywood of No. 41 High Street, (7) Mr Neame. Mr Webb was known to my family as 'dear old Mr Webb' and was the warden of the St Nicholas Almshouses at Harbledown. I believe he previously ran the bakery at No. 26 Orchard Street, St Dunstan's, which in my time was owned by Daniel Easton.

2: Childhood in St Dunstan's

This picture and my portrait on the front cover were taken at Stringers Studio when I was two years old. Below: St Dunstan's in my childhood. My favourite sweet shop, run by Sarah Welsh, can be seen on the corner of North Lane.

I WAS born on October 26, 1913 'above the shop' at No.7 St Dunstan's Street, Canterbury, where my parents were in business as bakers and pastrycooks. In earlier years this part of the street, between the Westgate Towers and Station Road West, had been called Westgate Street, usually abbreviated to 'Westgate.' During or perhaps just before my childhood Westgate Street became part of St Dunstan's Street but the old name lingered on and even as late as 1929 we were still, quite unofficially, giving our home address as 'No. 7 Westgate.'

My father bought the bakery from R.W. Whittaker, whose name can be seen above the shopfront in photographs taken at the turn of the century. In Mr Whittaker's day the shop was called the Westgate Bakery — painted in big letters on the front wall between the top floor windows — but when I was a little girl the name was no longer used and everyone knew the shop as 'Nicholls the bakers.'

My earliest memory is of being carried around our living room on the shoulders of a soldier who was billeted with us during the Great War. Our gramophone, which had a big red horn, was playing a marching tune. I was told later by my mother that the soldier was Jewish, that his name was Symmons and that he was later killed in France while on active service.

West Gate and Flagstaff, Canterbury

The West Gate.

Two views of the Westgate, soon after my father took over the bakery in 1907. The top picture, from a Valentine's postcard, shows strollers and shoppers on a sunny afternoon. No. 7 St Dunstan's is depicted when Dad was halfway through having the front wall repainted. His name is now on the top floor but has yet to replace that of R.W.Whittaker above the shop window. In the other picture, from a coloured postcard in Raphael Tuck & Sons' 'Oilette' series, we see a delivery boy carrying what is probably a basket of muffins past our shop.

My second memory, which is not quite so clear, is of looking out of a window, I think at night, to watch an airship — perhaps a Zeppelin — passing overhead. I also have a vague recollection of seeing wounded soldiers from France in their blue uniforms resting on the pavement in St Dunstan's, waiting for ambulances to take them to hospital.

My brother Harry remembers more about the Great War, as he is three years older then me. He recalls how the lights flickered and the windows rattled when the guns opened fire during the Battle of the Somme; it is an established fact that the bombardment could be heard in Kent.

Harry also remembers a German Gotha bomber crashing in Broad Oak Road, on the outskirts of Canterbury, early one morning in December, 1917.

When the war was over Mum asked Florrie Austen, her assistant, to take us out to see the lights in all the shops and houses, which had been observing the 'black out' for so many years. I was five years old and Harry was eight.

☐ ☐ ☐

I can still remember many of the other shopkeepers and residents who were in St Dunstan's in my childhood. Although I lived

"Our gramophone was playing a marching tune."

16

The 15th century *Falstaff Hotel*, our 'next door neighbour,' in the days when the bakery at No. 7 St Dunstan's (on the right of the picture) was still run by R.W. Whittaker. I'm sure that the bread barrow parked outside was among the equipment that went with the business when Dad bought it from Mr Whittaker in 1907. I enjoyed many rides home on that barrow when Dad and I had finished our rounds. Further up the street are the *George & Dragon* pub at No. 13 and various shops, including that of Dad's friend Edward Simmons at No. 14 and, at the far end of the row, George Wheatley's newsagent's and tobacconist's shop, where I bought my comics.

surrounded by sweets at No. 7, I always went along with my pocket money to Sarah Welsh's very popular tobacconist's and confectionery shop at No. 5, on the corner of North Lane, to buy sweets as she had such interesting ones – gob stoppers, sherbet dabs, liquorice allsorts and liquorice pipes, and packets of sweet matches or 'bunkers,' made from toffee.

She displayed all these delightful things in a corner at one end of her window. I would run along to Miss Welsh's every day to see what new treats she had; most of them would cost me a ha'penny or one penny She sold ten Woodbines for fourpence, ten Players for sixpence, and a box of 50 Players for half-a-crown (2s 6d).

She was probably related to the Welsh brothers who ran a carriage works just round the corner from her shop, at No. 3 North Lane; their signboard was above her shop window.

□ □ □

Our next-door-neighbours were Nash & Co., 'military tailors, breeches makers and ladies' costumiers' at No. 6 and the *Falstaff Hotel* at Nos. 8 and 9. I went in there a lot because two of my friends lived there; they had scooters and we would ride them down the middle of the road and go really fast. The hotel had a 'bat and trap' club and on Saturday evenings in the summer we could hear them playing in the hotel garden, which was next to our back yard.

The hotel has changed hands many times over the years. It had a bar where the main entrance is now and I would lie in bed and hear the customers merrily 'turning out' at 10 o'clock.

Just past the *Falstaff* were Robert Butler's barber's shop at No. 11, Charles Skam's house at No. 12, the *George and Dragon* pub

Tradesmen on their rounds in the St Dunstan's area in the 1920s. Dad is seen with his bread barrow and basket in Salisbury Road, and Mr Tharp, our milkman, has parked his cart outside our shop and can be seen in the doorway. There was no bottled milk in those days. Customers brought jugs to their front doors and they were filled by Mr Tharp from his large brass churn, while his horse waited patiently to be told to 'gee-up' to the next customer.

and, at No. 14, Edward Simmons the tailor. Mr and Mrs Simmons were good friends of my parents and had four children — Naomi, Bob, David and Ruth. Mrs Simmons was a lovely lady, always smiling. Dad often went along to chat with Mr Simmons while he was sewing. Bob Simmons became very well-known in Canterbury, as the proprietor of a camera shop at No. 14 St Dunstan's and leader of the Blue Shadows dance band.

A few doors along, at No. 18, on the corner of Kirby's Lane, was George Wheatley, newsagent and tobacconist. I bought the *Rainbow* comic there every week and followed the adventures of 'Little Nell.' It was a long wait each week for *Rainbow* day. The *Schoolgirl's Weekly* was another of my favourites. The heroine of the stories was Betty Barton, and the nasty one was called Ursula. We took the *Daily Mail* and the *Sunday Dispatch*. Mum was

I still treasure a letter I received in 1929 from one of my childhood heroes, the Kent and England cricket A.P.F. (Percy) Chapman. I wrote and asked him for his autograph, giving my address as '7 Westgate' – even though it had long since been changed to 'No. 7 St Dunstan's Street.'

St Dunstan's Street as I first knew it. In the top picture Frank Durtnal, draper and milliner, stands in his shop doorway at No. 79. Two schoolgirls have just hurried past; the one on the right, in her straw hat, belted summer frock and black stockings, may well be me. A few doors along (beneath the sign advertising 'Tea Rooms') is William Peters' shop. A waggoner and cyclist head towards us, while across the street a few motor vehicles have parked outside the *Falstaff* and my parents' shop. On the left two ladies and a dog are crossing Kirby's Lane and may be about to call at George Wheatley's newsagents shop (on the corner). The next two shops along are W.T. Hadfield's bakery at No. 17 and Moys Bros' greengrocery. The middle picture features the west side of the street. Note the elegant electric street lamp in the foreground and the old gas lamps at the railway level crossing. The building nearest the camera is the *Rose & Crown* pub, next door to No. 75, David's Haircutting Salon (advertising 'Lloyds Gold Medal' tobacco at 4d an ounce). Fred Glover, the blind basket maker, lived at No. 74, then came Mrs Goldfinch's stationery shop and post office, St Ninian's School, St Dunstan's House (now the *House of Agnes* hotel and restaurant) and picturesque rows of shops and houses all the way up to St Dunstan's Church. The bottom picture gives a better view of the *House of Agnes* (Agnes Wickfield's residence in Charles Dickens' *David Copperfield*)

89   CANTERBURY. — The House of Agnes. — LL.

very fond of puzzles and crosswords and took a magazine called *Answers*. I don't think she ever won any prizes!

Sadly, Mr Wheatley was killed during an air raid in the Second World War.

Charles Marsh the fishmonger was at No. 20. There were no fridges, so pieces of ice were strewn over the fish. Huge blocks were delivered by a horse-drawn cart.

At No. 22, on the corner of Station Road West, was Percy

Lamb's millinery shop. Hats were big in those days, and trimmed with flowers and ribbons. Mum had little time to visit the shops, so when she needed a new hat I was sent along and Percy would give me half a dozen or so to take home for her to try 'on appro.' She chose the one she liked and I took the rest back.

The price of a hat would usually be five shillings and eleven pence three farthings! Nowadays, milliner's shops are hard to find.

Our greengrocer was Hope Nicholls, my father's brother, whose shop was at No. 27, next to the railway crossing. He and my Aunt Edith measured out potatoes by the pound in round wooden bowls and kept a block of dates on the counter, selling them for 4d a pound. I liked buying dates. Aunt Edith would cut them with a big knife. They were very sticky but had a delicious flavour — they always tasted better than boxed ones!

Hope had a smallholding in Salisbury Road and kept bees there. He had a big Airedale dog, Whisky. I was scared to death of him; he was certainly a good guard dog!

Across the road, at No. 51, on the corner of Orchard Street (virtually opposite Flint & Sons' St Dunstan's Brewery) was a butcher, Herbert Rigden. One of my school friends, Rosie Bentley,

Main picture: this shop by the level crossing in St Dunstan's was my Uncle Hope's greengrocery shop, though it is seen here some years earlier when Edmund Burley traded there as a pork butcher and greengrocer. Note the tiled front wall and the auctioneers' advertisements on the side wall. Above: my Aunt Edie and Uncle Hope in their tiny garden alongside the railway.

London Road, as I knew it in the days when I went this way to St Dunstan's School, a few yards beyond the trees on the left. I often visited No. 9 London Road, the third house on the right past the lamp post in the foreground, to see my friends Marjorie, Eileen and Vera and their foster mother, Mary Austen.

lived nearby at Vine House, No. 44 Orchard Street. Mr Rigden's slaughter house was behind his shop. I shall never forget seeing the animals, mostly pigs, being dragged in by their tails to be killed; and hearing their terrible screams.

No. 65 was the home of Mr and Mrs Henry Nicholls (not related to us, as far as I know), who ran the toy shop at No. 91 before it became Mr Penney's fish shop. Their daughter Annette (Nettie) delivered bread for Dad, pushing one of his barrows.

My Grandmother Calver had a bed sitting room on the first floor at No. 65. I would sit with her at her window; there was always something to see, as the window overlooked the railway crossing.

In those days people often sat at their windows and 'watched the world go by.' Taking car numbers was a popular pastime among children.

As a treat I sometimes stayed the night with Granny – she had a comfy feather bed! She could make a hot drink on her coal fire but I used to take her a jug of hot milk from home every evening. Mum supplied her main meals.

Like all grandmothers of that time she was usually dressed in black; those who were over 70 were considered to be very old indeed.

Fred Glover, a blind basket maker, lived and worked at No. 74. He also mended cane chairs. He knew every inch of St Dunstan's. He would often be seen carrying a chair on his back. He always knew exactly where he was, and would walk straight to his door. Crossing the road was not a problem, of course, because there was so little traffic.

One of the most famous buildings on the west side of St Dunstan's is the *House of Agnes*, the home of Agnes Wickfield in Charles Dickens' well-loved book *David Copperfield*. It is now a hotel and restaurant. The exterior has remained the same since

21

This picture postcard puzzled me for many years after I bought it at a collectors' fair. Why are there two 'Union Jacks' on the Westgate Towers, both on the same flagpole? I think it is generally agreed that the flag at half-mast was raised when Queen Victoria died, and the top flag was raised for the proclamation of King Edward VII.

my childhood; inside there are floors at different levels, oak beams, inglenook fireplaces, low ceilings and many other period features.

Across the street from our house was Westgate House, home of the Misses Laurie. It must have had at least six bedrooms. They kept servants and had stables for their horses, and a very large back garden. As I mentioned earlier, there was a stone ball on the wall by the tradesman's entrance and it is still there today.

Immediately opposite our house, and next door to W. & R. Fletcher's butcher's shop, was William Penney, the fishmonger. The Penneys had seven daughters — Cherrie, Violet, Ivy, Nellie, Fanny, Dolly and Lilly. Fanny was my best friend; we were always together and always laughing, especially when she was teaching me to ride a bicycle. I spent some lovely times with the Penney girls.

At weekends Mr Penney would smoke herrings – naturally there was a strong smell! One of his customers was a Mrs Williamson, and I remember seeing her horse and carriage waiting outside Mr Penney's while she was buying fish.

□ □ □

My brother Harry and my aunt, Fanny Moore (née Calver), in St Dunstan's, c. 1922. W & R Fletcher's butcher's shop at No. 90 is across the street and Mr Grant, who worked there, is standing in the doorway.

A charming scene from a picture postcard published in the early years of this century by Noakes & Co., stationers, of No. 28 St Peter's Street. An elegant lady carrying her 'dorothy bag' approaches the St Dunstan's railway level crossing under the shade of her parasol. Children trot along the pavement behind her and a small boy at the corner of Station Road West gazes in wonder at the early motor car that happily does not appear to be frightening the horses drawing the traders' carts. The prominent advertisement proudly boasts 'Budge's for Boots' although by the time I came along some years after this picture was taken, the advertisement had been replaced by one for 'Teal's Corn Stores.'

Playing ball in our back yard.

No. 7 St Dunstan's was a big house, with five bedrooms. There was no bathroom; we had a big tin bath in front of the fire, which we filled with buckets of water carried from the kitchen.

There was no garden either — only a back yard. Dad's bread barrow and some tradesmen's bicycles took up most of the yard but somehow we managed to play cricket out there, near the 'coal hole' — and dangerously close to the bakehouse windows! Our part of St Dunstan's was very near the River Stour and I remember Dad sitting up all night when it flooded, watching the water rise in the cellar and worrying in case it reached the level of our electricity fuse box.

The shop at the front of the house had a big window on each side of the main door. In one window we displayed confectionery, and in the other bread and cakes. Inside there were four marble-topped tables where teas were served, and cases filled with chocolates – Cadbury's, Fry's and Nestle's. We sold bars of milk, plain and cream chocolate priced from 2d to 6d each and ½lb slabs for about one shilling (five new pence in today's money!).

Behind the counter were shelves holding round glass bowls of biscuits, bags of flour and, on the bottom shelf, dozens of glasses for soft drinks and ice-cream.

A pot of tea for two would cost about 4d; a cup of tea cost 2d. Sometimes, customers would order a pot or cup of tea and eat food that they had brought with them, even though a pot of tea, some bread and butter and one or two cakes would have cost them only a shilling.

In the summer, home-made ice-cream would be served at the tables – in glasses, or in a penny cornet or twopenny wafer. My

Many people but hardly any traffic are in this photograph of 'just another day in St Dunstan's,' taken in the late 1920s or early 1930s for a picture postcard published by Mrs A. Wildey, who had a bookshop at No. 2 Canterbury Cathedral Precincts. Our shop's blinds have been lowered to provide shade, or shelter from a summer shower, and two young men striding past our neighbours, Nash & Co., the military tailors, have noticed that they are being photographed. An open touring car has parked outside Kennett & Sons' furniture store, auction rooms and depository at Nos. 1 - 4 St Dunstan's, on the corner of North Lane.

mother and Florrie made the ice-cream in a tub filled with custard powder and milk. They turned the tub's handle by hand and the job took quite a while. The ice-cream was deliciously creamy. We did not have a refrigerator, so we had deliveries every day from the Canterbury Ice Works in Stour Street.

The cake window was full of home-made penny and tuppeny cakes and buns, Queen cakes, rice buns, jam puffs, currant buns and ginger nuts and muffins. I helped Mum make the ginger nuts. She mixed the ingredients into a bowl, rolled the mixture into strips and cut them into little squares, which I rolled into a ball and flattened with the palm of my hand. I loved that job.

The dough for the bread was made overnight, alternately by Dad and his assistant, Alfred Woodcock, who cycled to work from his home at Chartham. Jack Scott also worked with Dad in the bakehouse. I remember him falling down the steps which led up to the flour loft. I can see him now, smothered in flour – with his eyes just visible.

Over the years we had a lot of cats in the bakery. We needed them, and they had to be good mousers. When the lids of the dough troughs were closed, one of our cats would sit on one of them for hours, watching a mouse hole and catching the mice in his paw whenever they ventured out.

Black beetles were another pest. I hated them. They thrive in the warmth of bakehouses – at least, they certainly did in ours. I was afraid to go in there after dark.

An ice-cream mixer like the one we used at the bakery.

The opposite side of St Dunstan's from Mrs Wildey's picture postcard shows a fascinating assortment of carts and bikes outside Edward Wood's grocer's shop, the Gun Dining Rooms and Mr Penney's fish shop, whose signs tell us that he also had a branch at No. 35 St Peter's Street. The view allows us to peep past the Westgate Towers for a glimpse of an advertisement for the 'East Kent' omnibus company, whose 'road car station,' as it was then called, is just round the corner in St Peter's Place.

The bread varied in price. Farthings were then in use, so the price of a loaf would be 2¼d (tuppence farthing) or 4¼d (fourpence farthing). Bread was delivered daily, by Dad with his barrow and Alfred on his bike.

Their rounds were all over the St Dunstan's area – North Lane, Station Road West, Orchard Street, Roper Road, London Road, Forty Acres and Whitstable Road – and beyond as far as Harbledown and St Stephen's.

Sometimes Dad and Alf went a long way to deliver a small loaf or three pen'orth of buns. On Saturdays I would go with Dad on his rounds, and on the homeward journey I would have a ride on the barrow. I loved that.

We had a 'Saturday boy,' Ted Scoones, who recently told me that he remembers cycling all the way to St Thomas' Hill, while on his rounds for Dad.

□ □ □

I went to St Dunstan's School in London Road. Harry can remember taking me there on my first day. My teachers in the 'Infants' were Mrs Topliss and Miss Spillett.

Mrs Topliss had joined the staff as headmistress of the Infants' department in 1901, at the same time as her husband John became headmaster of the 'Mixed' school.

Our day-to-day journeys around Canterbury were made on foot or bicycle or by bus. Taxi-cabs could be hired for special outings from Arthur Skam of Oaten Hill Mews, whose parents lived at No. 9 St Dunstan's. The picture above was taken in St Peter's Place and shows some of my relations about to set off for a drive in what is probably one of Skam's cars. I recognise, from the left, (1) Vic Elgar, (3) Sally Tritton (my late husband's mother) and (5) Polly Elgar (Vic's mother). In the top picture one of the St Dunstan's area's few motor car owners, Mrs Henry Williamson of 'Bramhope,' is seen in Roper Road at the wheel of her Star limousine when she took part in a Canterbury carnival as 'Kent Hop[e]s.' The car's decorations include toy cricketers and scoreboards on the roof, an abundance of hop-bines, and a figure of an Indian cricketer on the bonnet.

St Dunstan's was often bustling with people making their way to and from Canterbury West railway station in Station Road West and the East Kent Road Car Company's bus station in St Peter's Place – providing our shop with valuable 'passing trade.' The bus company's Head Office and Central Works were in the Station Road West/ Kirby's Lane/North Lane area, only a few minutes' walk away, and many of their employees were regular customers. Here we see 'East Kent' office staff in Station Road West, ready to set off on an outing to Brighton on May 16, 1931. I am reliably informed that the two charabancs have Tilling Stevens B10D2 chassis and 30-seater bodies built by Shorts of Rochester! The picture was taken by B. & W. Fisk-Moore, one of Canterbury's best-known photographers.

□ □ □

I remember some of the interesting characters who often passed our shop. Very early in the morning I would hear a man wearing clogs approaching. He lived in Cross Street, and was walking to work at Williamson's Tannery in Stour Street. I could hear him coming down St Dunstan's from a long way off. Mr Silas Williamson, of the family that owned the tannery, lived at No. 59 London Road.

A man pushing a barrow would pass by, on his way to Whitstable to collect shellfish to sell in Canterbury. He walked there and back, a distance of about 12 miles.

Every morning the 'muffin man' would be heard ringing his bell in St Dunstan's Street.

Another well-known 'character' was Dan Sherrin, an artist from Whitstable. He was usually attired in a loud check suit and plus fours, and when he had a 'drop too much' — always during Cricket Week! — he caused quite a stir, shouting to all and sundry.

□ □ □

Like all shopkeepers in those days, Mum and Dad worked very hard. Mum was either busy serving in the shop or working in the bakehouse, where I would hear her singing 'The grandfather clock was too big for the shelf ...', 'You in your small corner ...', 'Father dear father, come home with me now ...', 'Poor cock robin...' and other songs that now always remind me of my childhood.

At weekends Mum 'did the books' until eleven or twelve o'clock at night. She suffered bad 'sick headaches,' especially on Sundays. Migraines were unheard of then, but I imagine a 'sick headache' was the same thing.

I have mentioned Mum's fondness for puzzles. She was also a great reader, one of her favourite authors being Ethel M. Dell.

I was very excited if she said she was going out, it was so un-

With George Coe, son of G.H. Coe, pastrycook, in 1920. George became a well-known dance band musician in Canterbury and his son, Tony, is a world-renowned jazz clarinettist and saxophonist. I am wearing my fur-trimmed coat and tam-o-shanter. When my mother first saw this picture she said that, had she known I was going to have my photograph taken, she would have 'tidied me up a bit!'

usual. Sometimes, after work, we would have a good look round the shops and occasionally Mum and Dad would go to the pictures, while Granny Calver looked after Harry and me.

On Saturdays I went shopping for Mum as she was always busy in the bakehouse or the shop. I always had to buy a pound of salt butter from Maypoles at No. 21 St George's Street and a pound of lean back rashers from the World's Stores grocery almost next door, at No. 24. On my way home I walked through the Longmarket and looked at all the stalls.

The bulk of the week's shopping came from Mr Lush's grocery shop in St Dunstan's. My purchases from Mr Lush usually included two pounds of granulated sugar, a packet of Brooke Bond tea, two pounds of soda, one pound of mild American cheese, plus from time to time two pounds of candles.

□ □ □

Like Mum, Dad enjoyed reading. His favourite author was W.W. Jacobs. Dad was very deaf and had a hearing aid. This was a very complicated contraption and used to confuse him, so he would take a candle up to bed and read his book there.

He loved watching cricket and playing bowls and was a great

Feasting on gooseberries in the garden of No. 9 London Road on Whit Monday, 1926, with Mary Austen's foster children Marjorie, Vera and Eileen.

My brother and I reading the *Sunday Pictorial* in our back yard in the summer of 1928, watched by our Aunt Fan. Cricket was front page news that day. We entered this picture, unsuccessfully, in the *Pictorial's* 'Happy Snaps' competition.

whist player; whist drives were extremely popular. I hated playing with him; I never did the right thing and he took the game very seriously.

When I was in my teens I used to play tennis with a friend on the Victoria Recreation Ground, and later with my future husband Ted. All sorts of events were held on the 'Rec': I remember a display by the 'Zulus' (blacked-up soldiers from Canterbury Barracks), firework displays and carnivals, usually during Cricket Week.

Canterbury Carnival was very popular and well supported. Many of the shops and businesses entered floats and one we always looked for was from Mounts the florist's, well-known all over the county for their roses. Their car in the procession would be completely covered with blooms. The Carnival Queen and her attendants were at the front of the parade and there were always two or three bands, probably the Buffs from the Barracks, the Sea Cadets, the Boys' Brigade, and sometimes some Scots Pipers.

Children from various streets would be there with their decorated scooters and bicycles, and two or three fire engines brought up the rear. The procession would take an hour or so to pass.

The streets were lined with spectators, three or four deep, and our windows would be full of our school friends — all of us were so excited, straining our ears to be the first to hear the drums. "It's coming, it's coming", we would say.

Men carrying linen bags on long poles would reach up to the windows and we would put our pennies in, or throw them on to a float. The Kent and Canterbury Hospital was always represented, with collection boxes, as it relied on voluntary contributions. Most shops had a 'hospital box.'

□ □ □

When I was about 10 years old there was an outbreak of scarlet fever in Canterbury. Epidemics of scarlet fever or diphtheria were common then and one year there were two children to a bed at the City Isolation Hospital in Stodmarsh Road.

I caught scarlet fever and had to stay at home for a while, probably because of bed shortages, but when I finally went into hospital I was taken there in the horse-drawn 'fever cart,' with blacked-out windows; I remember waving goodbye to one of our neighbours, Mrs Penney from the fish shop, as I was driven away.

By then I had got over the worst part of the illness and was in the 'peeling' stage. While I was away my bedroom was fumigated and sealed. We were kept in hospital for six weeks. No visitors were allowed and we had to talk to our mums and dads through a closed window.

A rare view of a window display in St Dunstan's Street in days gone by. William Peters ran a restaurant and tea room at No. 82 and was also a confectioner and baker. St Dunstan's Street was well served with bakers when I lived there. As well as my father and Mr Peters there were F.R. Fagg at No. 29 (near Flint's Brewery), W.T. Hadfield at No. 17 (only ten doors away from us) and C. Phillips at Nos. 41 and 42 (near St Dunstan's Church). Mr Peters has a fine assortment of sweets in his window, and advertisements for cocoa, chocolate, chops and steaks, pots of tea for 5d and 'Kop's Stout.' The window display next door features samples of wallpaper, a cross and a crucifix, since Mr Peters' neighbours, H. W. Bateman and Sons, were builders and undertakers.

Mum and Dad's shop (called the Chantry Stores) and house in Herne, c. 1937, where they spent the last years of their working lives. Popular brands of tea and cigarettes are prominently advertised, as is 'Bing', the flavoured mineral water that slaked many thirsts during the hot summers of the 1930s.

This was during the period when most people in St Dunstan's, when they were ill, were looked after by the 'Wacher doctors' – Dr Frank and Dr Harold (our doctor) – and Dr Stuart. Their surgery was on the King's Bridge, next to the Weavers.

Like all children, I was always falling over and cutting my knees. There were no handy plasters and the wounds had to be bandaged with clean rags. I will never forget the smell of Germolene ointment! It was agony having the dressings changed as they would always 'stick.' I screamed every time.

In those days we also had a 'nit' nurse who came to our school to inspect our heads. We had to stand in a row and bow our heads as she came along with her comb.

□ □ □

Some of my childhood memories are tinged with sadness. From the age of 12 until I was about 15 years old I would take three little sisters, Marjorie, Eileen and Vera, and their dog 'Trot,' out for walks. The girls were aged between three and five, and 'Trot' had a different bow for every day of the week. I pushed Vera in her pram. We often walked as far as St Lawrence Cricket Ground. The girls lived at No. 9 London Road (which still exists) with their foster mother, Mary Austen, an unmarried lady who was very deformed. She looked after the girls so well. Mary's garden was very overgrown and had many fruit bushes and trees, and she kept chickens there. The children lived with Mary for about five years. They were much loved and very happy until suddenly, one day, they were taken away by the fostering authorities. It broke Mary's heart.

Mum and Dad in their retirement, with my son Paul at Herne Bay when wartime barricades still disfigured the seafront.

□ □ □

Looking back to my childhood and life in Canterbury between the wars, these are some of the things I miss seeing and experiencing today:

□ High perambulators, with babies sitting up comfortably and looking around at the world. Prams in the 1930s were so well sprung and easy to push. Ted and I bought a beautiful 'Silver Cross,' which cost five guineas, for our sons. Luxury!

□ Being able to leave babies in their prams in the front garden for an hour or two, looking out now and then to make sure they were happy but never having to worry for a moment that they would come to any harm. Mothers would also leave their babies in their prams outside the shops, making sure of course that the brakes were on. Such things are certainly not possible today.

□ Men always walking on the outside of the pavement, raising their hats to all the ladies, and also when a funeral procession passed by.

□ The two minutes' silence on November 11 when everything, even the horses and carts and motor traffic, stopped. I am so pleased that this simple way of honouring the memory of lost fathers, sons and brothers may be revived.

□ The street cry of the 'rag and bone' man.

□ Council workers clearing the snow from the pavements.

□ Horses moving slowly along the snow-covered streets, with their hoofs bound with rags to prevent them slipping and their drivers walking alongside, holding the reins.

□ Horses with nose bags, feeding in the streets.

□ Early closing day, when all the shops shut at lunchtime on Thursdays.

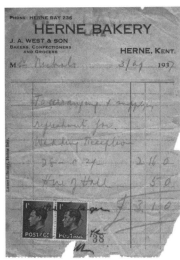

The bill from our wedding reception caterers when I married Ted Tritton at Herne n June 3, 1937. 'To arranging and supplying refreshments, £2.16.0. Hire of hall, 5s. Total: £3.1.0.' Below: one of the joys of shopping today: a clear and detailed bill from the check-out.

```
        SAFEWAY
     lightening the load


GET YOUR LOTTERY TICKET FROM THE KIOSK
    AND BE A WINNER WITH SAFEWAY

    Customer Services Manager
          MARTIN FULLER

  Your checkout operator today was
              MICHELLE
                                       £
  1.71 lb @ £0.25 /lb
       POTATOES NEW LOOS.         0.43
       ORANGES EACH              0.19
  0.57 lb @ £0.99 /lb
       GRAPES WHT LS             0.56
  0.79 lb @ £0.49 /lb
       BROCCOLI SPEARS           0.39
  1.12 lb @ £0.25 /lb
       CARROT LS                 0.28
  0.79 lb @ £0.39 /lb
       APPLES GOLD/DEL LS        0.31
       S BAC/GRILLS CHS          0.99
       NSTL KIT KATX8...         0.85
       S A/PURP CLOTHX10         1.35
       S FARMHOUSE BREAD         0.39
       S F/C TRIFLE STRWB        0.42
       S F/C TRIFLE STRWB        0.42
       LOS BA LIVE YOG           0.51
       S F/C TRIFLE STRWB        0.42
       HAM ON THE BONE           0.86
       S DOUGHNUT                0.38
       MATURE WHITE CHE          1.50
       S GINGER NUTS             0.39
```

☐ Shop window displays with hidden numbers, to encourage 'window shopping.' Those who found the numbers were rewarded with a prize.

☐ The peace and quiet of Sundays, when most people went for a walk. Ted and I did, usually to Blean or Harbledown.

☐ Mincing the meat 'leftovers' to make Shepherd's Pie, using a mincer which you clamped to the kitchen table. Nowadays, minced meat is sold at the shops, ready to use.

☐ Housewives outside their front doors or in their gardens, beating their carpets.

There are, of course, many aspects of present day life which compensate for the things I miss, among them the smile and cheerful 'Hello' that greet me when I arrive with my shopping trolley at the check-out in our big stores. I approve of the name-badges the staff wear, telling me that 'Margaret,' 'Audrey' or 'Sharon' is seeing me safely past the till. We seldom know their surnames, whereas when I served in a shop I was always 'Miss Nicholls' to my workmates; Christian names were used only outside working hours. The check-out staff never seem to get flustered! I also appreciate the very detailed bills you receive, setting out the date and time and the price code of every purchase. Unlike not so many years ago, changing items or refunding cash is never any trouble.

At my local supermarket, Safeway, in St George's Place, I know all the staff and they make it a pleasure to shop there; everyone appears to be enjoying their busy jobs, even the hard-worked trolley man!

We left St Dunstan's in 1936, when I was 23 and had been working at Gouldens, in Canterbury High Street, for eight years. Dad sold the bakery to Alf Woodcock, who had been his assistant for many years. Mum and Dad moved to Herne where they bought a general shop in Herne Street.

When they eventually retired they moved to a semi-detached house called 'Tresco' in Lower Herne Road. It was the first time they had lived in a house without a shop. They were very happy there, as there was a garden — something they never had before.

Dad went blackberrying and mushrooming but never really stopped being a baker, as he used to help out at a local bakery. He died on June 10, 1943, aged 65. I think they had a happy married life; a life of hard work, well done.

They made many friends, especially during their years in St Dunstan's, and are remembered with great affection. People still say to me, 'I remember your Dad's cakes and buns.' All this was very long ago but is still vivid in my memory.

After Dad died, Mum moved back to Canterbury and lived in a row of pretty cottages in Old Dover Road. They would be treasured today but were demolished some years ago. Later she came to live with me and Ted in St Lawrence Road, where she died on November 15, 1972, at the age of 92.

Ted Scoones, who has been a friend of mine since we were at school together, has kindly written down his childhood memories of St Dunstan's and neighbouring places for me and has allowed me to publish them here:

"I was born on October 19, 1912 at No. 48 North Lane and my first memory is of a German Zeppelin flying slowly over Canterbury in 1918. During the First World War air raid warnings were given by the Police by raising a red flag on the Westgate Towers.

"On this occasion my sisters and I were playing on the Victoria Recreation Ground. Mother had to come and find us and we got back to the Westgate as the Zeppelin passed overhead.

"At this time Forty Acres (at the top of St Dunstan's) was a field, fenced around and used as a prisoner of war camp. We used to see the prisoners on our way home from school.

□ □ □

"I remember the big flood in Canterbury in 1928. There was an earlier one in 1909. My father married my mother at Sellindge that year and when they came back to our home he had to wade up North Lane carrying her!

□ □ □

"When I was about nine years old I joined the St Dunstan's Church Choir, and remained a member until the Second World War. Mr Nicholls sang tenor in the choir: we had 14 boys, 10 men and about 15 ladies, four of whom were contraltos.

"Mrs Henry Williamson of 'Bramhope,' London Road, was of much help in St Dunstan's Parish. She sang contralto in the choir and her gardens were always available for fetes and parties.

"I also remember Rosa Salvatori and her barrow, selling ice

Ted Scoones today and (opposite page) as a Cub with the 2nd Canterbury Scouts, *c.* 1921. Below: St Dunstan's Street from the Westgate in August 1997. Most of the buildings I saw from here when I first went 'up the towers' nearly 80 years ago have survived. The restaurant on the corner of North Lane (right, foreground) was Sarah Welsh's sweet shop.

cream in the summer and roast chestnuts in the winter at the Westgate.

"When I was 12 I started working on Saturdays for Mr Nicholls, delivering bread. In the morning I used a bicycle with a very large basket on the front. I first delivered in London Road and then made a second journey, up Whitstable Road.

"In the afternoon Mr Nicholls loaded up the large bread barrow and we delivered to Forty Acres, Mandeville Road and Roper Road.

"I think his pride and joy was making a very large loaf, decorated with a sheaf of corn and placed on the altar table at St Dunstan's Church for the harvest festival.

☐ ☐ ☐

"In 1925 I was Confirmed. In those days the yearly Confirmation Service was held in the cathedral, and all the city and country churches took part. There were about 500 boy and girl candidates. It was a most impressive service, as at that time the altar was at the top of the steps to the Quire – when we turned round we saw a mass of faces looking up at us from the Nave.

☐ ☐ ☐

"In 1926 I started an apprenticeship with S.W. Bligh in North Lane. He was a founder member of the British Broadcasting Company. When he left the King's School he joined the family coachbuilding business, Bligh Bros., in St Radigund's Street. He left there to start up on his own at Nos. 1 and 2 North Lane, converting car oil lamps into electric lamps.

"At this time he must have had a gift and foresight for wireless. In 1927 he made the first-ever portable radio set and presented it

Below: my favourite picture of the Westgate and my parents' shop, giving a delightful impression of our window displays. 'Toby' Nash (1891 - 1960), the famous watercolourist, painted this for me and my brother for 12s 6d and it was our Christmas present to our mother in 1933.

to our present Queen's father, when he was Duke of York.

"When his father, King George V, made his first Christmas broadcast there were very few wireless sets, so Mr Bligh made one available in the cathedral, which was packed to hear the King's message.

□ □ □

"I remember the St Peter's Cinema (the 'Canterbury Electric Theatre'). It was on the corner of St Peter's Grove, behind Longley's pork shop. The cinema moved to St Margaret's Street in about 1930. The building later became the Marlowe Theatre, which later took over the Odeon Cinema (previously known as the Friars Cinema).

"The old St Peter's Cinema was converted into a dance hall by Mr Fullagar, S.W. Bligh's brother-in-law, and was called the Odeon Hall.

□ □ □

"In my early days there was a fire tender and steam pump in Palace Street. This was drawn by two horses and owned by Sun Insurance. It could be used only by those whose property was insured with the 'Sun'.

"The public fire service was run by the Police. The Police could volunteer to be both policemen and firemen. They had bells fitted in their houses, operated from the Police Station in Pound Lane by a magneto. When the bell rang they had to report to the Westgate Towers, where there was a truck loaded with hoses, a standpipe, and also an extendible ladder. These they had to push and pull to the fire!

"In 1924 they had their first Ford 'T' fire tender, which was kept in Best Lane. There was one problem. No one could drive it! An Inspector had a go but did not manage the arch in the Westgate and stopped in the horsetrough!

"After a new front had been fitted a civilian was taken on as driver and caretaker of the equipment. Hence early pictures show Police at a fire, and one man (the civilian) wearing a brass helmet.

"The Chief Constable was in charge of the Police and the Fire Service, and the Auxiliary Fire Service, until the National Fire Service took over during the war."

Three small boys pose with their hoop and hobby horse outside Westgate House, St Dunstan's, in the days when there was no motor traffic and the street was a safe playground for children.

3: Beyond the Westgate

Below: the fascinating world that awaited me when, as a little girl, I ventured past the Westgate Towers into Canterbury's busy shopping centre. On the left, at Nos 39 and 40 High Street, is Gouldens' shop, where I started work when I was 15. Note the handsome lamp posts, the shoppers' smart hats and, across the street, the Guildhall's attractive window boxes. Although this picture was published by Gouldens a few years before I was born, the High Street looked like this throughout my childhood, the only big change being the decline of horse-drawn traffic and the advent of motor vehicles.

ST DUNSTAN'S was my 'village'; beyond the Westgate Towers is the City, with its own selection of fascinating shops.

St Peter's Street is the first street you come to and at No. 37 was Thomas Knowler Tritton's shop. Thomas, my husband Ted's great uncle, sold stationery, newspapers, tobacco, sweets and toys. Naturally, I liked the toys best. The shop was like fairyland at Christmas — lovely dolls, prams, train sets, drums, boxes of bricks, and fairies for the top of Christmas trees, all glittering in the window lights.

Sadly, not many people put fairies on their Christmas trees these days.

The toys were so well made then — they would last for generations — and the dolls' houses were delightful, with miniature furniture, made from celluloid or wood, not plastic.

I had a celluloid baby doll and another doll, which I named Betty Margaret. She had a china face and said 'Ma-ma'. Florrie Austen knitted a dress and hat for her; I had her for years.

At No. 51 St Peter's Street were Field and Jordan, the ironmongers. The shop front has not changed much over the years. It was truly a shop which sold everything. Whatever you couldn't get anywhere else, you would find at 'F&Js.' Pots and pans, pails, brooms, paraffin, oil, baskets, china, string, paint, nails – you

name it, they had it. About the only thing they didn't sell was elbow grease, though plenty of youngsters were sent there on a fool's errand to buy some!

I enjoyed visiting the shop — I liked the smell of the paraffin and string. Ernest ('Ernie') Jordan served behind the counter.

Once you cross King's Bridge, over the Stour, you leave St Peter's Street and are in the High Street, where I used to shop at the Penny Bazaar — a very long, narrow shop. Nothing cost more than a penny. It is now a card shop but otherwise it is almost exactly as it was, although the original counter has disappeared.

Baldwin & Son, at Nos 32-33 High Street, sold clothes, hats, sheets, tablecloths, as well as the usual haberdashery. I can remember the ladies' corsets, boned and shaped, drawn in tight at the waist, with laces at the back which were pulled to 'shape' the customer. It's a wonder she could breathe!

Upstairs was the millinery department. Hats were large, trimmed with ribbons, many of them priced at five shillings and eleven pence three farthings!

I was fascinated to watch customers paying for their purchases. Their cash and bills were put into a wooden container suspended on an overhead wire, and the shop assistant pulled a handle to send it whizzing above our heads to the cash desk.

There, the cashier took the money and sent a receipt and any change back to the counter in the same way.

I think the only other shop in Canterbury with this device was Deakins the outfitters, in Guildhall Street.

When my cousins Doris and Harold Smith came to stay in Canterbury we would always visit the Beaney Institute and Public Library, opposite Baldwins.

There were two fierce-looking stuffed animals in the entrance hall. One was a lion, showing its teeth. We always put our hand in its mouth. I think the other animal was a tiger.

They stood at the top of some stairs which led down to a basement room full of animal exhibits. It was a dark place. Under one display case, half hidden, was a crocodile which scared me to death; there were also snakes in jars, amongst other things.

I was quite glad to get back upstairs, though we liked the cases of birds and butterflies.

The Beaney Institute, where I encountered such frights and delights as snakes in jars, fearsome stuffed animals and a huge selection of library books. This view, from a Raphael Tuck picture postcard, was probably photographed from the first floor of the *County Hotel*.

□ □ □

Then, as now, the busiest place in 'the Beaney' was the Public Lending Library, which I joined when I was quite young. The Librarians were Len Butcher and H.T. Mead. The system for issuing books was different to the one we use today. You didn't see the book you wanted until it was handed to you by the Librarian.

First, you looked through a catalogue and noted the number of the book you wanted to borrow. You then went to a row of large upright glass cases, displaying coloured tickets bearing the numbers of all the books in the catalogue.

Red tickets indicated books that were 'out.' If the number you had chosen was on a blue ticket you were in luck — your book was 'in' and you could ask the assistant to get it for you from the back room where the books were kept.

Thomas Knowler Tritton's shop at No. 37 St Peter's Street. The toys and fancy goods in his window always fascinated me, and here we see his well-stocked display of newspapers and picture postcards. He was, though, a strictly religious man and would not sell Sunday newspapers! One of the advertisements beside his window announces the opening concert of the season of the Masqueraders Concert Party. The building was once owned by Huguenot weavers and the double door in the gable was used when their goods were hauled up from carts parked in the street below.

Today, of course, you can select books off the shelves, browse around, or simply sit and read and take your time.

Further up the High Street, past the Guildhall, was the Theatre Royal, where Debenhams is today. I think the theatre was later converted to become part of Debenhams, because I cannot remember ever seeing it being demolished.

I did not go to the theatre very often, except to see a pantomime once a year.

Opposite the theatre, on the corner of Guildhall Street, stood the Guildhall. Many people think it was demolished unnecessarily after the war. It was the centrepoint of many important occasions.

When you reach the corner of Mercery Lane, the High Street leads on to The Parade where, on the left, you came to the Longmarket, a name which well describes its layout.

There were stalls on each side of a long, covered arcade, selling all sorts of goods, as street markets do today.

Dad took us to the Longmarket on Saturday evenings and often bought some sheet music – usually priced at sixpence – for me from one of the stalls, as I was learning to play the piano.

Ernest Jordan's sister, Louise, was teaching me at her home in St Dunstan's Terrace. I went there once a week and made satisfactory progress. I liked playing but hated theory, which I used to try and 'get out of' and leave until the last minute.

Eventually I sat for the usual exams and passed one or two, but I always failed in theory. By the time I was in my teens I could play reasonably well, but I wasn't gifted enough to play 'by ear'. I would like to have been able to sit down and play whatever was requested, without having to take my music with me!

Playing 'by ear' was taboo with music teachers, but the really gifted pianists are those who can play anything asked for.

I still have some of the music that Dad bought me in the Longmarket. My mother bought pieces of china and glass there. After our Saturday evening out, Dad would buy Harry and me a bag of roast chestnuts.

Opposite the Longmarket was Baker's Temperance Hotel. This was owned by my father's step-brother, Alfred Baker, though I cannot remember ever going inside.

Beyond The Parade is St George's Street, which I remember as being very busy and narrow. It was the last street before you left the old city, though we seldom ventured this far from St Dunstan's.

Once we had walked as far as The Parade we had found somewhere to buy everything we needed.

□ □ □

Some impressions written in November 1992, some 70 years after the Canterbury shops previously described existed.

"Canterbury is going through a facelift — for the better, we hope. In 1991 the Longmarket's ugly post-war shops were demolished and the Canterbury Archaeological Society organised a 'dig' on the site, which lasted some months and caused much interest. Much was discovered — no graves or skeletons, but the remains of various houses and shops and the names of traders of long ago.

"The Roman Pavement was left intact but heavily covered for protection. It had been on public display for some years.

"The new development has been a great feat and when finished one can appreciate the thought that has gone into the architecture — gabled roofs, chimney pots, attractive lighting and lamp posts. Some of the units have now been occupied by Our Price and the Sweater Shop, to name but two, and attractively fitted out.

"The public have not yet seen the first floor of the development, but it has a courtyard (a quiet place to rest after shopping) overlooked by some shops and flats."

□ □ □

It is a very attractive scheme throughout. Time will tell if it will be a trading success.

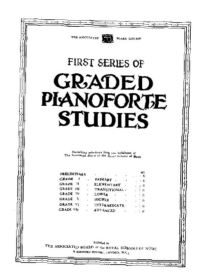

4: Among my favourite places

The Greyfriars, once the home of the Franciscan brethren. Hidden away behind Stour Street, this picturesque monastic building is just off Canterbury's tourist trail and is one of the city's 'best kept secrets.' I was delighted to discover recently that it is now open to the public on summer afternoons. My schoolfriend Irene Smith lived nearby in Franciscan Gardens, where her father John ran a florist's shop and nursery.

CANTERBURY was full of fascinating places where children could play and go exploring.

One of them was Whitehall, by the river, where Harry and I and our friends would watch the horses being washed in the Horse Pond, by the Westgate Gardens. Further along there was a stream full of tadpoles, which we would collect with our nets and jam jars. Harry remembers that one day I fell in the stream and emerged covered with weeds and slime!

We often walked down Whitehall Road as far as the railway crossing, where we crossed over to the 'ABC steps' (there must have been 26!) which led us to Mill lane and London Road. From there we would walk home. It must have been at least three or four miles.

On another of my frequent walks I would turn right when leaving our shop and pass Station Road West and my Uncle Hope's greengrocery shop at No. 27 St Dunstan's Street. I then turned into Roper Road, named after the Roper family. Margaret Roper, Sir Thomas More's daughter, lived hereabouts. Nothing is left of her house except the gateway. The adjoining building was a brewery when I lived in St Dunstan's.

On the right hand side of Roper Road I passed some of the many allotment gardens to be found in this part of Canterbury, and at the end of the road I turned left into Beverley Road (previously called Hanover Road) and walked on to Forty Acres, where Mount's nursery — famous for its roses — was situated.

My friend Lilian Vissenga lived at No. 20 Roper Road. I loved going to her house as she had a pianola, the first I had ever seen. It was magical to see the keys playing themselves!

Looking from her window I could see the railway station, usually with a Whitstable train in the foreground, waiting to depart.

We also often visited the Dane John Gardens, where the 'beadle' kept order. He walked around wearing a top hat and carrying a cane and tried to stop us climbing the banks, which were steep and fun to roll down!

We would also play hide and seek around the war memorial, and climb 'the mound' for a splendid view of Canterbury.

At that time the moat alongside the city wall and the Dane John, built for the defence of the city, was still in its natural state; it disappeared long ago to make way for the ring road. There were peacocks in the moat, and we would hang over the wall and wait for them to show their lovely feathers.

Sometimes we had a long wait!

At night, when all was quiet, we could hear their cries as we lay in bed.

Concerts were held in the Dane John Gardens in an attractive band stand, and during Cricket Week coloured lights were strung along the paths.

The Dane John has hardly changed and still has its avenue of trees and well kept flower beds. New railings and entrance gates have been erected and have greatly improved the approach to the gardens, in which major restorations are currently being carried out.

My cousins Harold and Doris Smith often came to stay with us and we always liked to go 'up the Towers' (the Westgate); I think the entrance fee for children was tuppence.

The visit started with a climb up steep, winding stairs, holding on to a rope. We arrived at the top feeling quite giddy! First we went into the room which houses the condemned cell, with instruments of torture on the walls. We could see some writing on one of the walls, which we were told was done by a prisoner.

There were ancient guns and suits of armour to look at, but the bit we liked best was getting to the top and looking at Canterbury from on high.

Florrie Austen would stand outside our shop and wave to us. I was, and still am, scared of heights, so I was always glad to return to the safety of St Dunstan's Street.

What a shame that Canterbury's other old gateways — St George's, North Gate, the Riding Gate and so forth — were demolished.

One of my school friends, Irene Smith, lived in the Franciscan Gardens in Stour Street, where her father John ran a florist's shop and a nursery business.

We had some lovely times there. The River Stour ran through the gardens and there was a boat in which we used to play — but we were never allowed to untie it from its mooring because the river was dangerously deep.

There were two bridges from which we used to try and catch fish. From one of the bridges there was a fine view looking towards King's Bridge and some lovely old buildings, including Assisi Cottage which was the home of William Smith.

The Grey Friars once had a monastery there. The chapel they built over the river can still be seen.

Alf Woodcock, my father's assistant for many years, pictured in 1955. Alf bought my parents' bakery when they moved to Herne in 1936.

Florrie Austen, who was my mother's assistant at the bakery and one of my best friends, pictured on the sea-front at Whitstable. Florrie married Gus White who worked at the Co-op in St George's Street. They lived in Old Park Avenue.

5: Easter and Christmastime

Below: a winter evening in St Dunstan's, from a picture postcard published by Charles Worcester & Co. The street lamps have been lit by the lamp lighter, whom I used to watch as he cycled past our shop, stopping at each lamp to reach up with his hook and pull the chains that regulated the gas supply to the mantles. The lamps within the *Falstaff* and our shop, and in the houses opposite, shine out to light the way home for the lone carter and for the few people who have ventured out as storm clouds gather above the Westgate Towers.

IT is the evening before Good Friday in 1930 and Dad and Alf Woodcock are preparing for a night of hard work in the bakehouse. By hand alone they will make hundreds of spiced, buttered and currant varieties of penny and ha'penny hot cross buns, all marked with an 'X.'

By 6 o'clock in the morning the buns will have been baked and brought into the shop to be put into bags, on which Florrie Austen has written the customer's name and the quantity required.

Orders have come in for six pen'orth or three pen'orth of buns and they will be delivered, still warm, before breakfast, by Dad and Alf in the bread barrow or in the baskets on their bicycles.

Harry and I, and some school friends, will help by walking to our customers, carrying our heavy but delicious-smelling baskets.

Mum has cooked a ham joint, and a good breakfast will await us on our return.

But the day's work will not end then. Although the shop will be closed, the bakehouse and the baking trays will have to be cleaned and Dad will wash the oven with his scuffle, a mop made of rags attached to a very long handle.

Florrie will sweep and tidy the shop, ready for opening the next day. The blinds will be drawn, the shop door locked, and in the evening the dough will be made for the bread to be sold on Saturday.

Hard work, well done.

☐ ☐ ☐

At Christmas I always think back to Christmases in the 1920s. The pace of life was much slower in those days and people had more time to stand and look in the shop windows, adorned with home-made decorations, coloured crepe paper, cotton-wool snow and paper lamp shades.

In the 'sweet window,' one of our two large shop windows, we would display boxes of crackers (2s each); boxes of 'Queen Mary,' 'King George' and 'Red Rose' chocolates (5s for a 1lb box, 2s 6d for ½lb); pink and white sugar mice (2d each), sugar fancies shaped like watches and animals, and chocolate 'smokers' outfits' — all surrounded by robins in the snow. Hanging from the ceiling there were stockings full of confectionery and novelties, priced at 2s, 1s and 6d.

In the other window, the 'cake window', we would put cakes of all sizes made by my mother and father, priced from five shillings; each one had a red frill and a robin on top.

There were also mince pies, ginger nuts in a round glass bowl, and all kinds of cakes and buns — Banbury cakes, Queen cakes, 'naps,' jam doughnuts, jam puffs, and so on — all at ½d, 1d, 2d or 4d. Only a few things cost more than tuppence.

On one of the white marble-topped tea tables stood an oil lamp with a red glass globe, which gave a lovely glow and also warmed the shop. This lamp was always a source of wonder to me, as it cast pretty patterns on the ceiling.

On the counter were a set of weights and burnished brass scales (one for sweets, the other for biscuits and flour), and the shelves were lined with jars of biscuits and sweets — humbugs, Sharpes toffees (2d a ¼lb), pear drops, 'winter warmers', mint lumps and liquorice allsorts.

During Christmas week, customers brought their own home-made cakes to be baked. It made a lot of extra work as it meant going to the bakehouse from time to time to check every one. On Christmas morning customers brought their turkeys and chickens to be cooked. I think we charged them 2d for cakes and 6d for turkeys.

We also made Christmas puddings and it was my job to remove the stones from thousands of raisins — a sticky job, which I did not enjoy.

Extra loaves had to be baked and delivered by foot, bicycle or barrow.

All this baking and cooking meant that our Christmas Day started very late but I never heard my parents complain, as all the customers were friends.

It was hard work but all done with good spirit.

I remember it is Christmas Eve.
It is midnight, the shop is closed,
the blinds are down.
Work is finished for another day.

As I lie in bed I hear the policeman on his beat,
trying all the doors;
making sure all is secure.
A lovely comforting feeling.

Dad on his rounds in Salisbury Road. His basket is empty, suggesting that he has just delivered some loaves and pastries – or maybe some hot cross buns or a Christmas order. Among his regular customers in this area were Mr and Mrs Frank Menniss at No. 11 Hamburgh Villas (now No. 28 Salisbury Road) – which is probably the house in the background – and Fred Noakes at Beaconsfield House, on the corner of Beaconsfield Road and Salisbury Road.

During Christmas week I had been sent to Uncle Hope's greengrocery shop to buy our Christmas fare — two pounds of mixed nuts, a dozen oranges, two pounds of apples, a box of dates, a box of figs, two pounds of tangerines and some grapes. All this would cost about £1. Grapes were in the shops only at Christmas, whereas nowadays you can buy them at any time of the year.

□ □ □

Our living room was decorated with home-made paper chains, holly over the pictures and a small but real tree with a fairy on top.

Among our presents would be a book for me, perhaps the *Schoolgirl's Own Annual*, as I had the comic each week and followed the serial adventures of Betty Barton.

One year Mum made me a doll's bed out of a chocolate box. It was lined with pink silk and contained a tiny celluloid baby. I loved it.

My brother Harry had a steam engine, with a boiler and an oil lamp underneath. One day it caught light and had to be taken out to the back yard pretty quick! Harry liked taking things to pieces to find how they worked, especially watches!

He was also very good at making things. When I was about 12 years old — this would be in 1925 — he assembled a crystal wireless set. I can see him now with his ear phones, fiddling with the 'cat's whisker.' It was a success!

We were all able to listen to 'the wireless' for the first time in our lives but because Dad was so deaf he had difficulty in hearing anything. The first things I heard over the air were the chimes of Big Ben.

In about 1925 we listened to 'the wireless' for the first time. In those days, most people tuned-in to the BBC's broadcasts on crystal sets and heard the programmes on headphones.

My Aunt Edith and Uncle Hope and my cousins Margaret and Jack would come to tea, probably on Christmas Day, and we would visit them on Boxing Day. We enjoyed that very much.

After tea we would play records on the gramophone. Military bands were a favourite, and Dad liked Harry Lauder. The grown-ups would play whist while we younger ones played Snakes and Ladders or guessing games.

Consequences was another favourite. We all had paper and pencil and had to write something down, turn the paper over to conceal the writing, pass it around, and read it out when it had circulated for a while.

Some very funny things were written: 'Mr So and So '... ' met 'Mrs So and So'... 'a t the gasworks' ... 'He said to her' ... 'She said to him' .. and so on.

Harry and I enjoyed the short walk home at midnight. It was an adventure to be out so late.

St Dunstan's Street is dark and quiet.

Christmas is over.

Happy New Year.

6: Cricket at Canterbury

'O my Chapman and my Woolley long ago!' A sight that stirred the hearts of cricket lovers in the 1920s: Frank Woolley and A.P.F. (Percy) Chapman walk out to bat for Kent at the St Lawrence Ground during Canterbury Cricket Week. The pavilion clock tells us that it is a minute or two past 11.30 – start of the day's play – and we see a police constable heading towards the boundary after clearing a way through the crowd of spectators for the batsmen. I took this photograph in 1929 on my first 'Box Brownie' camera.

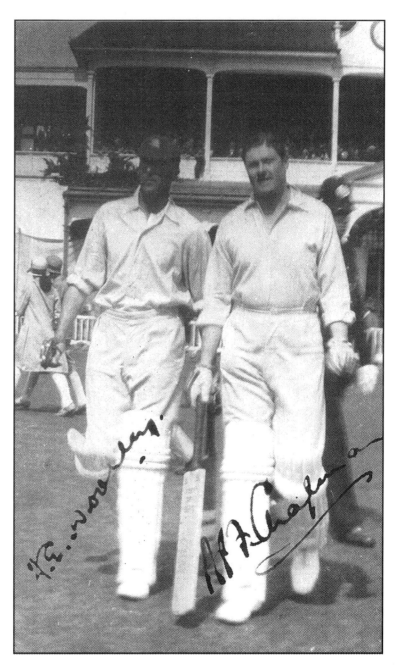

I HAVE spent many happy hours at St Lawrence Cricket Ground, some when I was young and many more as I grew older. Dad, Harry and I were keen supporters of Kent County Cricket Club.

One of my friends, Evelyn Bowen, came with me to the county matches and one day we went to Hythe, just to look at A.P.F.

Frank Woolley (left) and Arthur Fagg coming out to bat for Kent at another pre-war county championship match at St Lawrence. As usual a friendly crowd gathers round to chat to the fielding team and wish the batsmen good luck. Above: the letter I received from my hero Percy Chapman in 1929.

(Percy) Chapman's house! Cricketers as well as film stars were our pin-ups.

Chapman was very popular; he was tall, good looking, with fair curly hair. He fielded at silly point and was a good batsman. He played for Kent hundreds of times and became the team's skipper in 1931, having already been captain of England. Other members of the Kent first eleven when I was a girl in the 1920s were Frank Woolley, Leslie Ames, 'Tich' Freeman (a 'googly' bowler), Harold Hardinge, W.H. Ashdown, G.B. Legge and C.S. Marriott.

I have an autographed photo of Chapman and Frank Woolley coming out to bat, which I took with my Brownie camera. I sent a copy to Chapman and received a letter of thanks from him.

In Cricket Week we took our sandwiches to the cricket ground and stayed there all day. Our usual viewing point was on the boundary near the Old Dover Road entrance. It was close to the players, and easy to run on to the outfield to watch the team come in and out and perhaps get an autograph.

There were no advertising boards around the boundary then, and we were allowed to sit on the grass, five or six rows deep.

Joe Murrin, the groundsman, would come out and ring a big hand-bell when play was about to begin; schoolboy scorecard sellers walked around shouting 'scorecards, full bowling analysis,' and the Band of The Buffs played at the Nackington end during intervals in play — 'White Horse Inn' was a popular selection.

Ladies' Day was a real event, with very smart ladies parading during the lunch and tea breaks.

When the cricket season was over I often sat on one of the

At St Lawrence Cricket Ground on May 31, 1997, with (on the left) Evelyn Goddard (née Bowen), who first came to the ground with me more than 70 years ago, and (on the right) Ellen Fuller (née Jones). The picture was taken when Ted and I celebrated our Diamond Wedding with a family party at the Chiesman Pavilion.

benches at the St Lawrence ground with my school friends, recalling the matches of the past summer. I never thought that one day I would live almost within a fielder's throw of the pitch. It is a much-loved place for me. I have taken my children, grandchildren and great grandchildren over there, to play in the summer and gather chestnuts and conkers in the autumn.

St Lawrence is often spoken of as the loveliest cricket ground in England. I always think of it with affection, and I hope to go there for many more years to come.

□ □ □

Poems about cricket have always appealed to me. One of my favourites was, I think, published in *The Raj Quartet* by Paul Scott. It contains these evocative lines, based on At Lord's by Francis Thompson: *"It is little I repair to the matches of the Yorkshire folk ... though the red roses crest the caps, I know ... and a ghostly batsman plays to the bowling of a ghost .... as the run-stealers flicker to and fro ... O my Chapman and my Woolley long ago."*

□ □ □

When I lived in St Dunstan's, Canterbury Cricket Week was a full week, unlike today. It was always a busy time. The streets would be decorated with flags and fairy lights and our shop did a roaring trade. Many visitors came by charabanc to see the cricket and alighted in St Dunstan's before catching a bus to St Lawrence or setting off on the long walk to the ground.

Others arrived at Canterbury West railway station. But however they arrived, many of the supporters passed our shop on their way to the cricket and called in for refreshments; sometimes we were so busy that we had to open our private sitting room for the overflow. Some customers even sat on our stairs.

Most people ordered a cup of tea, price 2d, served in big, thick Willow Pattern cups. As soon as I arrived home from school I would start washing up.

I don't know why, but I never liked serving behind the counter; yet when I went to work as a shop assistant at Gouldens I wasn't at all nervous.

49

Cricket today is a very different game to the one I knew when I started supporting Kent 70 years ago. Then, the highlights of the season in Canterbury were Cricket Week (when two three-day county championship matches were played) and a visit from the overseas touring team. Today we also have 'limited over' one-day matches, with their own rules and tactics. My brother Harry took this picture at one such match at the St Lawrence Ground, as a fielder made a smart return to the wicket-keeper. What would the likes of Frank Woolley and Percy Chapman have to say about white cricket balls, black sightscreens and the players' colourful attire? Nevertheless, a day 'at the cricket' is still an exciting occasion and there is no better place to be than St Lawrence on a summer afternoon, among an appreciative crowd of spectators relishing the prospect of an exciting finish. And some things never change: St Lawrence's old lime tree still stands inside the boundary, and the rules still give four runs to any batsmen who hits it.

There's a breathless hush in the Close tonight –
Ten to make and the match to win –
A bumping pitch and a blinding light,
An hour to play and the last man in.
And it's not for the sake of a ribboned coat,
Or the selfish hope of a season's fame,
But his Captain's hand on his shoulder smote –
'Play up! Play up! and play the game!'

'Vitai Lampada' (1892)
© SIR HENRY NEWBOLT

7: At school at St Dunstan's

In the playground at St Dunstan's School, c. 1925. Left to right, back row: (1) 'Sid' Wallis, (2) Ruby Hadlow, (3) Lilly Cogger, (4) Winnie Port, (5) Lilly Coultrip, (6) Dorothy Browning, (7) Mary Nicholls, (8) Irene Smith, (9) Edith Couter, (10) Helena Cannon, (11) Evelyn Belsey, (12) Grace Burville; front row: (1) unidentified, (2) Gordon Richards, (3) Bill Beaumont, (4) Jim Goddard, (5) 'Pickle' Lilley, (6) Wilf Fassum, (7) Cecil Dorrington, (8) unidentified, (9) Charlie Voice, (10) Ted Scoones, (11) Fred Croucher. The building on the right in the background is the 'Post Office Telephonic Repeater Station' in St Dunstan's Terrace, which I believe was still being built at this time by George Browning, whose sign can be seen behind Evelyn and Grace.

I STARTED going to St Dunstan's Infants School, in London Road, in 1918, when I was five years old. When I 'passed up' to Senior School my teachers were Mr Topliss the headmaster (later succeeded by Joseph Daniels), 'Moggy' Atkinson, Mrs Filmer and Miss Chinery. I left school at 15.

I remember my school friends with affection – Rose Bentley, Evelyn Belsey, Evelyn Bowen, Grace Burville, Edie Couter, Evelyn Easton, Ella Inge, Ellen Jones, Fanny Penney, Irene Smith and many others.

Nothing very noteworthy happened to me at school. I wasn't particularly bright: no good at arithmetic, sewing or geography and only 'fair' at cookery, but I loved English composition, which was my best subject.

For school I wore a dress over petticoats and awful-looking bloomers — fleecy, lined ones in winter. When I was very young I wore a Liberty bodice over my vest, with buttons down the front, and buttoned boots. Mum fixed them with a button hook and I was always afraid it would pinch me!

When the school had its first uniform — caps or hats, and blazers with the school's first badge, a chalice — one girl and one boy had to parade in the classrooms, wearing the items. The girl was me, and the boy was Ted Tritton, my future husband. We were in the same class during my last term. He was brainier than me, good at maths and woodwork. His best friend at school was Norman Young.

The cane was much in evidence. Boys were given six of the best for misbehaviour, often for playing truant. Ted was caned twice —

for playing truant to visit a circus, and for roller skating outside the school during break.

On Empire Day we all marched through the streets for a service in the Cathedral. Beforehand we had a practice march in St Dunstan's Terrace, saluting the flag.

The school sports were held on the nearby Victoria Recreation Ground: football and cricket for the boys, stoolball for the girls. I was captain of Red House.

We had several playground games. In one of the most popular ones we formed a ring, with one girl in the centre and one outside. We then chanted:

> Lucy Locket lost her pocket,
> Kitty Fisher found it;
> Not a penny was there in it,
> Except the binding round it.

The girl outside would run around the ring saying 'It wasn't you ... it wasn't you' and then slap one of the girls on the back, saying 'It was you". That girl then had to race round, chased by the others.

Another of our games was 'statues.' One girl stood with her back to the others and they had to try and reach her before she looked round. When she did look, everyone had to stand as still as a statue. Anyone seen moving was 'out'.

Skipping ropes were much in evidence, as were spinning tops which we used to colour.

Every day we had 'drill,' which in the 1920s became known as PE. It was all 'arms stretch, knees bend,' and so on, performed in the playground. Primary schools did not have gyms.

In Senior School we performed plays in St Dunstan's Parish Hall in Orchard Street, and in the grounds of 'Bramhope', Mrs H. Williamson's big house at No. 56 London Road (now the Pilgrims' Hospice). They were usually plays by Shakespeare and I am

St Dunstan's Senior School pupils who took part in a performance of *Twelfth Night* at 'Bramhope' (now the Pilgrims' Hospice), London Road, in August 1928. Left to right, standing: (1) Les Cole, (2) Albert Bentley, (3) Dorothy Davis, (4) Ellen Jones; seated: Mary Nicholls; front: (1) Albert Johnson, (2) Cyril Relf.

St Dunstan's Senior School's stoolball players at a match at the Victoria Recreation Ground in 1929. Left to right, standing: (1) J. B. Daniels (Headmaster), (2) M. Paine, (3) D. Oliver, (4) D. Pearson, (5) I. Cook, (6) D. Gurr, (7) D. Mullaney, (8) M. Baker, (9) F. Penney, (10) M. Hutchings, (11) E. Clements; seated: (1) D. Goodwin, (2) M. Pearson, (3) P. Garner, (4) E. Solly, (5) Mary Nicholls, (6) Mrs Filmer (teacher), (7) E. Jones (team secretary), (8) D. Davis, (9) C. Hubbard, (10) E. Bowen; front: (1) L. Cogger, (2) I. Herman. Another of our players, E.C. Bennett, was not present when the picture was taken. In the background are some of the houses in London Road.

grateful to my friend Ellen Fuller (née Jones) for writing down these memories of our performances for me:

"I was a newcomer to St Dunstan's when we performed part of *King Lear*. Winnie Streeting and I played the two wicked sisters who 'conned' Lear to dispossess his youngest daughter Cordelia, the beautiful one. Mary was Cordelia and I think that Ted Tritton was the Earl of Kent and Roland Young was one of the other earls. Mr Daniels announced from the stage that all the costumes were made by the pupils. The boys made their shields and armour from cardboard and silver paint, and very realistic they were too.

"The performance was voted a great success, so six months later we did another, this time a piece from *Twelfth Night*, at Bramhope. I think we understood this a bit better: *King Lear* was heavy going for 13 year olds! *Twelfth Night* had more fun to it. I was Malvolio, the vain major-domo of the household of Lady Olivia, the beautiful owner of the house. We had a wonderful time with this one. Mary played Olivia, who was being wooed by Malvolio, who imagined that she was in love with him. The other children in the cast were Dorothy Davis (playing Maria the maid), Leslie Cole as Sir Toby Belch and Cyril Relf as the fool. This time we hired our costumes from Ovendens, the theatrical costumiers in Orange Street."

St Dunstan's School still stands and although the building is now a residential dwelling the facade is unaltered. The tree we played around is still in the playground and the inscription 'Infants' remains visible on the school porch.

I can remember every word of the Grace which we said before going home to lunch (or 'dinner' as we called it):

Be present at our table, Lord;
Be here and everywhere adored.
We creatures bless and grant that we
May feast in Paradise with Thee.

After this we made a noisy exit!

Happy school days, more than 70 years ago. I keep in touch with Ellen and Evelyn but sadly some of my school friends have passed on. Ellen is a marvellous artist in water colour and oils. I have some of her pictures on my walls.

Elsie Epps, Evelyn Easton, Ella Inge and I attended St Dunstan's Sunday School and, when we were older, we went to Miss Pittock's Bible class in Whitstable Road. We had 'best coats and hats' for Sundays.

Every year in the 1920s there was a Sunday School treat. We all met at Canterbury West Station for a trip to Whitstable. The fare was about 4d. return.

The journey itself was an adventure, especially when we entered the tunnel near Tyler Hill Halt. It was quite long and we had to close the windows, otherwise we would have been covered in soot — though sometimes we left them open just for fun!

My Great Aunt Eliza lived in a cottage at Tyler Hill level crossing. I'm not sure if it was the crossing keeper's cottage, but she always came out and waved to the passengers. I was very proud to say, 'That's my Aunt Eliza'.

It was a single line to Whitstable and the journey took about 30 minutes. On arrival we were taken to Tankerton Slopes, overlooking the sea, for games and races. If we liked, we could go to the beach and paddle, and walk along the stretch of shingle called 'the Street,' which was uncovered at low tide, looking for winkles.

The highlight of the day was a winkle tea near the harbour. We were each given a pin to get the winkles out of their shells.

I saved up about 1s. 6d. for the outing and spent most of it on ice-cream cornets (1d each) and rides on the swing boats (2d) but I always bought a present for Mum – an ornament, perhaps, or a string of beads.

There was an amusement arcade, with a machine in which you put a penny and saw a man hanged! Then home again after a very happy day.

In 1998 I revisited St Dunstan's School, 80 years after my first day there. The school is now an attractive residential development but most of its original late Victorian buildings survive. Above left: at the main gate in London Road. Above: the entrance to the Infants' classrooms. 'Beginners' went in through the door at the top of the steps behind me; another door in the porch led to a classroom for older children. The two rooms were divided by a sliding partition.

Cars and waste containers occupy what was our playground, but the trees under which we posed for our school photo more than 70 years ago (see page 51) are still there.

8: Sundays and special days

St Dunstan's Church Choir in Mrs Henry Williamson's garden at 'Bramhope,' London Road, c. 1927. Mrs Williamson is sitting in the centre of the picture next to the Vicar of St Dunstan's, Rev. E.L. Ridge. My father, Fred Nicholls, is standing immediately behind and between Mr Ridge and Mrs Williamson. Ted Scoones is standing seventh from the left in the back row, and his sister May is fifth from the left in the front row. The ladies are wearing splendid examples of hats of the 1920s!

THERE was a certain 'feeling' about Sundays in St Dunstan's. The shop blinds were down, the sun would filter through, and all was still and quiet.

I would climb into the 'cake window' and clean all the glass and shelves. Afterwards I usually walked to the cemetery with flowers to put on my Aunt Kate's grave.

It was a common sight in those days to see people taking flowers to the cemetery; cremations were very rare.

The bakehouse oven was not fired on Sundays and because Mum had no oven in the kitchen — only a gas ring — our Sunday dinner was fried bacon and eggs, which we all enjoyed. I especially liked the Clipper dried peas she served with the 'fry up.'.

It seems strange to me now, to think that Mum had to cook everything in the bakehouse oven – such a lot of trotting to and fro.

As I mentioned earlier, I attended St Dunstan's Sunday School. I also went to Holy Cross Church for Evensong with Mum, while Dad went to St Dunstan's Church.

The boundary between the two parishes crossed St Dunstan's Street; our part of the street, once called Westgate Street, was in

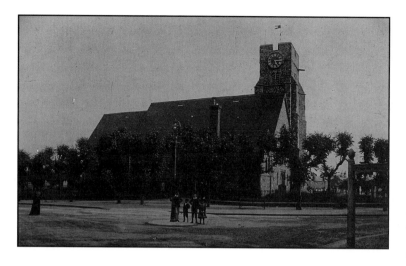

This photograph of St Dunstan's Church, from a picture postcard by Noakes & Co., reminds me just how deserted and peaceful this corner of Canterbury was on Sunday afternoons. The churchyard is shaded by pollarded trees, and the smartly-dressed children are standing where today a 'mini-roundabout' controls traffic milling around the junction of Whitstable Road, St Dunstan's Street and London Road. Note the old sign on the right pointing to Whitstable, our destination for many walks and seaside trips.

Holy Cross parish, while the section from Station Road West northwards was in St Dunstan's parish.

The services at Holy Cross were rather dreary; a small congregation, and always the same people sitting in the same pews.

I remember seeing Mr and Mrs Thomas Tritton, Ted's relations, and their daughter Florrie; Mr and Mrs Waterfield, who had a jeweller's shop in St Peter's Street; Mr and Mrs Horsley (a lovely old couple); the Prett family; and Mr and Mrs Saunders from the bakery in St Peter's Street.

From where Mum and I sat I could watch a boy pumping the organ, and see Cyril Relf, a choir boy I fancied! The organist was Violet Saunders, like me a baker's daughter.

St Dunstan's Church had a larger congregation. Dad was in the choir. He was very fond of music and loved listening to military bands and Harry Lauder. He was one of the choir's tenors. I can see him now, walking up St Dunstan's Street to morning service, with his straw hat and silver-topped walking stick. which I still have.

Sometimes he would bring members of the choir back to our house to practise for a church concert.

My brother Harry belonged to the Canterbury Cycling Club and was miles away at weekends!

Yes, Sunday was different; a special day.

□ □ □

We went to some good concerts at Holy Cross Parish Hall. The church choir would take part and Mr Coombs, a baritone who always had a solo spot, would sing 'Watchman, what of the night?'.

The Crotchets' dance band would play and was very well received; a real sensation. The leader, F. Norris, was a brother of a member of the choir, and gave his services free. The hall was always packed.

St Dunstan's Church held concerts in the parish hall in Orchard Street, and they too were well attended.

May and Doris Scoones gave dumbbell displays, May played the mandolin and the choir and its soloists would sing.

9: Golden days at Gouldens

The picture below speaks for itself of happy days at Gouldens in the 1920s and 1930s. I am on the far left with (from the left) Eunice Weatherall (stationery department), Irene Huntly (fancy goods department) and Clara Brickenden (cashier). The photograph was taken in about 1934 in White Horse Lane, near the shop's goods entrance, where we spent much time larking about and taking 'snaps' of one another on our 'Box Brownie' cameras.

I HAVE only to mention 'Gouldens' to my contemporaries and they say 'That was a *lovely* shop.' It was a family-owned business, situated at Nos. 39 and 40 High Street, where Pizza Hut and Vision Express are today. My cousin Margaret Nicholls, who ran the stationery department, helped me get a job there in 1928, when I was 15. I served in the Christmas card department, where my boss was Joyce Savery.

The prices of the cards started at between 1d and 6d. They were laid out for sale on trestle tables. Each one had to be priced individually. We must have sold hundreds. We had to find the right envelope for each one.

Newcomers were always taken on in the Christmas season, hoping that they would be kept on in the new year. I was one of the lucky ones. I was transferred to the stationery department and stayed there for nearly nine years, until I left to be married.

My boss in Stationery was Dora Kennett, who had taken over from Margaret. Dora was a first class worker who really knew the stationery trade. She was very strict and we often had a 'grumble' about her – but she trained us well..

Business hours were 9 am to 6 pm on weekdays (though on Thursdays we closed at 1 pm) and 9 am to 8 pm on Saturdays; in Christmas week we were often open until 9 in the evening. Before we opened all the assistants had to take turns in sweeping the shop floor, which would not go down too well today.

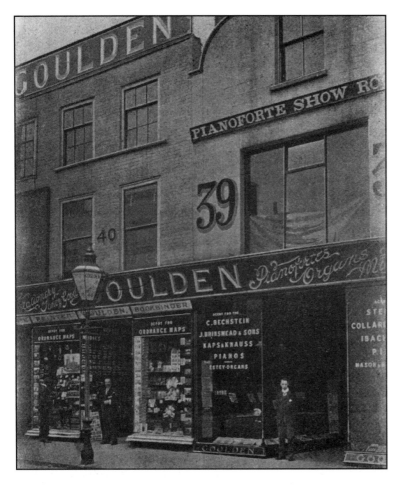

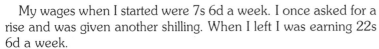

Left: Gouldens' shop at Nos. 39 and 40 High Street, as I knew it when I first went shopping with my parents in Canterbury. By the time I joined Gouldens in 1928 the music shop, which sold pianos, organs and sheet music, had moved a few doors down the street to No. 36, on the corner of White Horse Lane. This allowed the stationery, fancy goods and book departments, and the lending library, to expand and take up the whole of Nos. 39 and 40. In the windows on the left a fine display of postcards and books has been arranged to entice shoppers. Above: a later view of No. 39. The cyclist is passing Dollond & Aitchison, the opticians, and heading towards the corner of White Horse Lane.

My wages when I started were 7s 6d a week. I once asked for a rise and was given another shilling. When I left I was earning 22s 6d a week.

As you entered the shop, Stationery was on the left and took up the whole length of the shop, which was very long. Turning to the right you were in the department that sold books, greetings cards and calendars, and the lending library.

On the right-hand side, opposite Stationery, were travel goods, handbags, gifts, glass and pottery, followed by hymn books, bibles and artists' materials.

Toby Nash, a local artist, painted pictures which were sold in the shop – all Canterbury views, showing the Cathedral, the Weavers, and so on. He was a marvellous artist, not really recognised in his life time, but his work is much sought after now.

Mr Gontran Goulden had his desk in the centre of the shop and was always available if a customer wished to speak to him. His little dog, Pip, who was just like the one in the HMV Gramophone advertisements, came in every day and sat beside him.

The stationery department was very busy; each assistant had her own stock to look after and had to see that the cupboards were kept full. I started with ink – 'Stephen's' in blue, black, red and green, and 'Parker's' in the same colours, and also purple. There were dozens of sizes in 3d, 6d, 1s and 2s 6d glass bottles, and large stone bottles which must have held two pints. There was also special ink for marking linen. Each bottle had to have a price ticket

Right: Nos. 39 and 40 High Street today. Pizza Hut takes the place of the music shop and Vision Express sells spectacles where I served stationery. The cyclist is passing the passage that led to Gaywood's Restaurant. 'My' top stockroom was on the top floor of No. 39 and our staff tea room was on the top floor of No. 40, behind the central and right-hand windows. The first floors of both buildings were mostly stockrooms. There were no lifts: all incoming goods had to be carried upstairs, and carried down into the shop after they had been sorted and priced. The stationery business was sold to Hatchards after Gontran Goulden retired in 1949 but Leslie Goulden continued to run the music shop, which survived until the 1960s.

put on it — and the tickets weren't self-adhesive!

The ink stock was kept in the cellar, next to the boiler room. Reams of brown paper were also stored there; my job was to separate and fold them into single sheets, to sell at 2d to 6d each. We stocked 50 sizes of manilla envelopes; customers would buy large ones separately;.

There was a very wide range of writing paper, boxed and in pads, in two or three sizes, with smooth or matt surfaces. Some of the brands were Basildon Bond, Itona, Kings Castle, Rose Arch (deckle edged), Hieratica (black bordered), Pepys, Waldorf Club, Boswell Bond and Crown Bond.

If the customer wished, we would split up a box and take perhaps half or three quarters of the sheets up to the binding and die stamping room, put it into a large machine, and cut them up into smaller, single sheets. The binding room was up two flights of stairs and through a trap door, but going to and fro with handfuls of stationery for our customers was all part of the service.

I quote from a booklet about Gouldens: "Steep little stairs and trap doors in the most unexpected places ... intricate winding passages and rooms at different levels ... like something out of a historic novel."

In those days, when a death occurred in a family, mourning

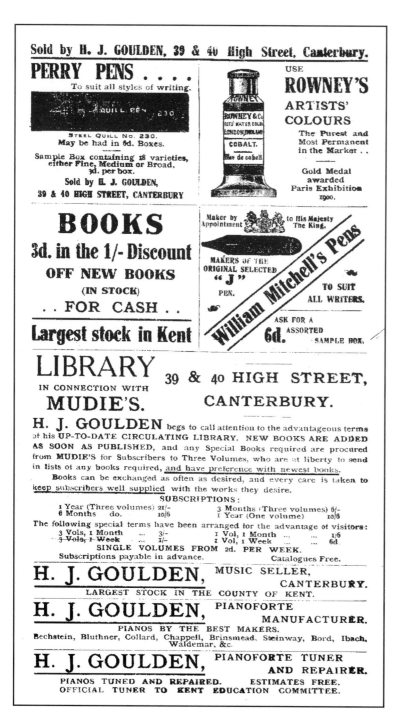

Above: Gouldens' music shop on the corner of White Horse Lane in the early 1950s. The window display includes sheet music and a selection of 78 rpm gramophone records. Next door to the shop are the Weald Furriers and the 'Sun Life' office.

Music shop assistants Celia Neaves (centre) and Joan Wallis (right) with Carrie Culver, who worked in the office, at the White Rock Pavilion, Hastings, during a staff outing in the 1930s.

stationery was used. This consisted of notepaper with black borders (narrow or wide), envelopes (also black-edged) and cards on which were printed the name of the deceased and an appropriate verse. After taking an order for an 'in memoriam' card I would have to check the verse by reading it to Dora. I am a little ashamed to say that we would often have a fit of the giggles, especially if the verse was very sentimental.

There was a large assortment of fountain pens in a glass-topped counter – Swan, Conway Stewart, Onoto, Watermans and so on, some with old-fashioned 'plungers'. A customer would usually ask to 'try the nib.' They often wrote their signature and that was how

Everyone who went shopping in Gouldens remembers the book department and lending library, situated at the back of the shop. From here a door led into a corridor which ran behind Nos. 37 and 38 High Street and into the music shop at No. 36. In the top picture, shop assistant Evelyn Newport stands behind a display of new novels. The poster under the clock advertises J. B. Priestley's latest book, Angel Pavement (one of my favourites), published in August 1930. The time is 5.20, so if it is a weekday there are only 40 minutes to go before closing time. In the picture below, Phil Nye and May Legge are at the same table but this time the advertisement under the clock is for Jane Austen's novels.

I obtained the autographs of Dick Sheppard, Dean of Canterbury, and Reginald Foort, the well known organist who came to Canterbury to play at the Regal Cinema. Pen nibs cost 2d or 3d each or you could buy a box for 6d.

It was 'please pay at the desk' in those days. We would make out a bill in duplicate, keep one copy, give the customer the other and ask 'Sir' or 'Madam' to pay at the desk and bring back the receipt before taking the item. Sometimes we would slip up and not ask for the receipt, and they would get away without paying!

The cash desk was in the centre of the shop — there were no individual tills as now.

Gouldens had customers of all classes. I remember a lady who used to say to the assistant, 'Now, I want your undivided attention.' Woe betide anyone who interrupted!

Another customer was an old gentleman who was very deaf. His hearing aid was a big horn which he held to his ear, and we had to shout down it — very embarrassing, because the shop would go very quiet while everyone listened.

Stationery department staff in the 1930s. Left to right: Kathleen Bennett, Winifred Over, Dora Kennett, Mary Nicholls, Eunice Weatherall.

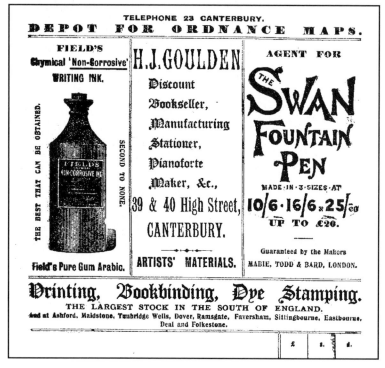

In Stationery we had a cubby hole, behind where the ledgers, typewriters and typewriting paper were kept. If an awkward customer came in, the assistants would make for it and leave someone — usually a junior, like me — to cope!

Another very demanding lady lived in the Precincts and was not easy to please. One day she left a cake behind by mistake. We kept it for a day and because nobody came back we ate it in the cubby hole. Then of course she came and asked us if she had left it. Nobody knew a thing!

Orders were delivered by bicycle: often it would be just a small packet, such as two toilet rolls. A customer would telephone for an item, perhaps as late as 5 o'clock, which was not popular with the delivery men, who rode around town on their trade bikes. The shop sent and received a lot of mail, of course, and after Christmas the postmen would call to collect their 'Christmas boxes.'

After a time I was elevated to 'table stationery,' which was kept

Gouldens' girls Dora Kennett (left) and my cousin Margaret Nicholls larking about in Baker's Yard, White Horse Lane. The *Fleur de Lis Hotel's* coaches and motor cars were kept in the yard, which was known as 'Baker's Yard' because Harry Baker, the hotel's coachman, worked there. He lived at No. 6 White Horse Lane, opposite the yard. The lane was a busy byway in the 1920s and 1930s, with people coming and going to Gouldens, the hotel yard, the *Fleur de Lis Tap* pub (run by Harry's brother Percy) and Bigglleston's foundry. On Sundays the lane echoed with the happy sound of services at the Salvation Army Citadel and you would see the Salvationists and their band marching home after their open-air meetings in the city.

at the top of the building. This stock included paper doilies in 20 different patterns and six sizes with serviettes to match. A customer would take some considerable time, choosing and matching each item. There was also a large selection of dish papers, pie dish frills, cake decorations — silver and golden for anniversaries, lovely gift boxes of doilies and serviettes, which would sell at 2s 6d to 5s.

The top stock room overlooked the Guildhall and was a good viewing point from which I witnessed many important civic events, including the arrival of Lord Baden Powell for the ceremony at which he was made a Freeman of the City in September 1930.

The Guildhall was demolished after the war, unnecessarily in the opinion of many people.

One of the stock rooms was at the far end of the shop and was presided over by 'Nunky' George. We had to climb very high ladders to reach the shelves, and cling on like monkeys to reach what we wanted. Goods for the stock room were delivered to the shop's rear door by Mr Howard of Suttons the carriers, of No. 6 St Peter's Street; Mr Howard's daughter Gladys worked in our office.

One day I was allowed to dress one of Gouldens' windows. The display was of china models of the Cathedral, the Westgate Towers and the Weavers. I was quite proud of my effort. I went to lunch and when I came back the whole display had crashed down;

everything was broken, including the shelf. I had placed the display items too close to the edge!

That was my first and last attempt to dress a window.

Gouldens also had a music shop, on the corner of the High Street and White Horse Lane. The shop's cellar was once a Royal Mint. Gontran Goulden's brother, Leslie, was in charge of the music shop, which sold pianos, gramophone records and sheet music.

It was the custom then for an assistant to sit and play the piano by the open door, to attract passers-by – much nicer than the 'canned music' that blares from some of Canterbury's shops today. It is a shame that a cathedral city allows this.

'Mr Leslie' gave talks on musicians – Beethoven, Bach and others — at Rotary Club lunches and other functions. Sometimes we would stay on after hours and he would give one of his talks to the staff.

Above the music shop there was a workshop where Ted Kennett was in charge of typewriter repairs, French polishing and other services.

My days at Gouldens were very happy. It was a family shop and we were all part of that family. Sadly, we will not see its like again.

This picture was taken a minute or two before or after the one on page 57, probably by Eunice Weatherall, whose place in the group has been taken by a colleague from the music shop.

Staff in my time at Gouldens
Stationery: Kathleen Bennett, Dora Kennett, May Legge, Evelyn
Newport, Mary Nicholls, Winifred Over,
Eunice Weatherall, George Young.
Fancy department: Betty Francis, Phyl Taylor and two others.
Books: Miss Archer, Phyl Nye.
Library:
Mrs Ginder, Mildred Ovenden, Kath Shoebridge.
Cards and calendars: Joyce Savery.
Office staff: Carrie Culver, Gladys Howard, Olive Kingston.
Music shop: 'Bob' Barwick, Kath Freeman,
Celia Neaves, Joan Wallis.
Workshop: Charlie Ashby, Ted Kennett.
Piano tuner: Mr Blackford.

Joyce Savery had many talents. She made flowers out of crepe paper and earrings from sealing wax, framed pictures with *passe-partout,* and coloured photographs (in those days cameras took only black-and-white pictures).

She was also good at waving our hair. We would come to work with straight hair and disappear up to the binding room, where she would be warming her curling tongs on the gas ring on which Lilly Stringer heated the glue for book binding.

Soon afterwards we would return to our counters with a lovely 'hair do' of waves and curls. I am sure 'Mr Gontran' noticed our disappearances and transformations but he never said a word!

Standing behind me in this picture taken near Gouldens' goods entrance are (from the left) Betty Francis, Phyl Taylor and Eunice Weatherall.

Before I joined Gouldens there was a staff outing, usually to the coast, on a Thursday, which was early closing day. In my time we had an annual staff dance at the County Hall (previously known as the Queen's Concert Hall and Ballroom), near St George's Church. It was destroyed in the Second World War.

□ □ □

We shop girls were very-fashion conscious in the 1930s and hats especially were chosen with great care.

The style I liked best were 'halos'. They had turned up brims and were worn tipped back to show the face. 'Cloche' hats were also very popular, as were fur tippets!

I remember going up to London on a Thursday afternoon with one of my friends, probably Eunice Weatherall; we had a great time trying on hats in 'C&A.' There were stacks of them, priced at 4s 11d.

Shoes usually had high heels — they were called 'court shoes'. I remember paying 4s 6d for a pair, and sometimes as much as 12s 6d!

Shoulder bags were uncommon; we preferred 'clutch bags' which you tucked under your arm or held in your hand. There was no fear of bag snatching in those days.

Stockings were made of silk and were very shiny, in ghastly colours. They had seams, which looked awful if they weren't straight.

We could wear what we liked to work (within reason!) and usually chose a navy or black skirt with a white blouse. One year in Stationery we decided to have a change. We each wore a bottle green dress, in individual styles, but I didn't much care for the idea and we soon went back to navy or black outfits.

□ □ □

One day a few months ago I paused opposite Nos. 39 and 40 High Street and looked up at the front window in what had been 'my' stock room at Gouldens more than 60 years earlier. I spent many hours in that room, attending to my 'table stationery' and also just looking out the windows! From the back I used to look towards Whitehall and its rows of poplar trees and beyond towards Chartham and Chilham. It was a fine view.

As I stood on the corner of Guildhall Street I remembered how I would watch the traffic in Guildhall Street entering the High Street and heading to and from Thanet and Herne Bay. Before traffic lights were installed, a policeman stood on point duty in the middle of the road.

Looking above the modern shop fronts that have replaced Gouldens' entrance I saw, to my surprise, two relics of the days when these streets were choked with motor traffic. There, on the wall above the shop windows, are signs identifying the street as the A2 and pointing to Chatham and Dover.

I walked into the passage alongside No. 40 High Street, which 60 years ago led to the side entrance to Gaywood's Restaurant at No. 41. Looking up at the side wall to No. 40 I saw the window to

(Continued on page 69)

Day trips from Canterbury for Gouldens' staff in the 1920s ...

Boarding a charabanc outside the shop for an outing in 1927. I recognise, from the left, (1) 'Micky' Payn, (3) Margaret Nicholls (looking ahead through the windscreen), (4) possibly Marjorie Monk, (6) Phil Nye (sitting by the door), (8) Carrie Culver, (9) Phyl Taylor, (10) 'Bob' Barwick (in profile), (11) May Legge, (12) Evelyn Newport, (13) Rose Hooker, (14) Mr Blackford (our blind piano tuner), (15) Mr Blackford's daughter, Connie. It is a Thursday (early closing day), the shop is shut and the blinds are down to shield the window displays from the sun. Note the variety of signs, including Gouldens' name on the street lamps.

The proprietors: Henry James Goulden (centre) with his sons Gontran (left) and Leslie. They have obviously decided that it is warm enough to shed the coats they wore during the journey from Canterbury.

Fashionable Gouldens girls cutting a dash in Tenterden during their outing in 1927. From the left: 'Bob' Barwick, Marjorie Monk, Phyl Nye, Phyl Taylor, Evelyn Newport, Celia Neaves, an unidentified colleague and May Legge.

Proprietors on the promenade. Henry Goulden with Gontran (centre) and another of his sons, Francis, during a staff outing to Hastings in 1925. Left: Another picture taken in 1927, showing Mr Leslie Goulden with his wife (standing on his right) and Gouldens' librarian Mrs Ginder, who had her own library in Canterbury before she joined Gouldens.

...they're off to the seaside, to sit on the beach and stroll on the prom

Truly one big happy family firm! Pictured here in 1927 are, left to right, standing: (1) Charlie Ashby, (2) 'Tich' Fagg, (3) Ted Kennett, (4) Dora Kennett, (5) Lilly Stringer, (6) Eunice Duffield, (7) Mrs Ginder, (8) Leslie Goulden, (9 and 10) Mr and Mrs Gontran Goulden, (11) Mrs Leslie Goulden, (12) Francis Goulden, (13) May Legge, (14) Evelyn Newport, (15) unidentified, (16) Mr Lightfoot (piano tuner), (17) Jessie (our tea lady), (18) unidentified, (19) Rose Hooker; middle row: (1) unidentified, (2) Marjorie Monk, (3) Phyl Nye, (4) unidentified, (5) Carrie Culver, (6) unidentified; front row: (1) Celia Neaves, (2) Margaret Nicholls, (3) Gladys Howard, (4) Phyl Taylor, (5) 'Bob' Barwick, (6) Joyce Savery, (7) Olive Kingston, (8) unidentified, (9) 'Micky' Payn.

Those pebbles were hard but we kept smiling! Left to right: Evelyn Newport, 'Bob' Barwick, Celia Neaves, Phyl Taylor.

Staff at Hastings in 1925. In the background Connie Blackford guides her father along the pavement outside the Queen's Hotel.

We may be at the seaside but we wouldn't be without our hats and fur tippets! Among those in this picture, taken in 1925, are, from the left: (1) Joyce Savery, (2) Margaret Nicholls, (3) 'Micky' Payn, (5) Eunice Duffield. Right: Leslie Goulden sets up his camera to make a souvenir cinefilm.

At a Gouldens' staff dance at the County Hall, St George's Street, Canterbury, *c.* 1930. I recognise (left to right, back row): (1) Celia Neaves, (2) Eric Elton, (3) Evelyn Newport, (4) May Legge, (5) Joyce Savery, (6) Dora Kennett, (7) Phyl Nye, (8) Arthur ('Tich') Fagg, (10) Harry Ashby, (11) Charlie Ashby; centre row: (1) Irene Vissenga, (2) Kathleen Shoebridge, (4) Rose Hooker, (5) Clara Brickenden, (6) Mary Nicholls, (7) 'Micky' Payn, (8) Eunice Weatherall, (9) Eunice Duffield, (10) Margaret Beech, (11) Lilly Stringer, (12) George Moxey, (13) George Young, (14) Ted Kennett; front row: (1) 'Bob' Barwick (almost out of view), (2) Gladys Howard, (3) ? Goldsmid, (4) Carrie Culver, (5) Olive Kingston, (6) Mrs Ginder, (7) Gontran Goulden, (8 and 9) Mrs and Mr Leslie Goulden, (10) Phyl Taylor, (11) Miss Harris, (12) Jessie, our tea lady. This was the second of several photographs that I have had published in the *Canterbury Extra* newspaper's *Memories* feature. The first was my picture of the Canterbury Master Bakers (see page 14), which launched the feature in 1984.

□ Mr and Mrs Henry Goulden had 14 children. I have already mentioned their sons Gontran (born in 1884), Leslie (b. 1894) and Francis (b. 1899). Their other sons and daughters were Charles (b. 1879), an opthalmic surgeon; Wilfrid, who died aged four months in 1881; May (later May Weeks), b. 1882; Nora (later Nora Twyman), b. 1885; Ida (later Ida Johnston), b. 1887; Daisy (later Daisy Kean), b. 1889; Leo, b. 1891, a solicitor; Christina (later Christina Chambers), b. 1892; Osmund (Leslie's twin brother), a barrister and teacher; Anthony, b. 1895, a shopkeeper in Tunbridge Wells; and Marjorie (later Marjorie Kempton), b. 1901. Francis ran shops in Hastings, Bexhill-on-Sea and Rye.

Left: these Gouldens girls formed a group called the 'Ukulettes' in the late 1920s. I recognise most of them. Left to right, back row: (1) Dora Kennett, (2) Marjorie Monk, (3) Evelyn Newport, (4) Phyl Nye, (5) D. Archer, (7) Celia Neaves; front: (2) Margaret Nicholls.

In April 1985 my Gouldens friends were reunited at my home in St Lawrence Road, nearly 50 years after I left the shop to get married. We realised that it was probably the last time we would all get together. Today only two of us survive. Top right: Evelyn Paine (née Newport) and me (standing), with (left to right) Olive Rogers (née Kingston), Gladys Browne (née Howard), Joyce Walton (née Savery) and Clem Nicholls (née Nye), Phyl Nye's sister. Right: May Hatch (née Legge), Phyl Mann (née Taylor) and Marjorie Young (née Monk).

Gouldens' staff meet again, after 50 years

Gladys and Leslie Goulden recall the good old days. May, Evelyn and Olive are also in the picture.

One of the old snapshots we passed round at our reunion. Taken in 1925 it shows Joyce and Olive (first and third from the left) with Margaret Nicholls, Lilly Stringer and 'Micky' Payn.

(Continued from page 65)

what had been the binding and die stamping room at Gouldens. From this window we would look down on the functions in the restaurant — a wedding reception, perhaps, or a party.

I then walked past Nos. 39 and 40 High Street to No. 37, which was the Weald Furriers, and No. 36, which was Gouldens' music shop. From here I walked down White Horse Lane, where we used to have our photographs taken. What with gazing out of the windows and posing for snapshots, it's a wonder we found time to serve the customers!

While poking around these passages and yards I was sorry to find that parts of this area are so devastated, dirty and in a poor state of repair. For example, the once beautiful bay windows to Gaywood's reception rooms were broken and falling to pieces.

I hope these buildings will not be neglected for much longer.

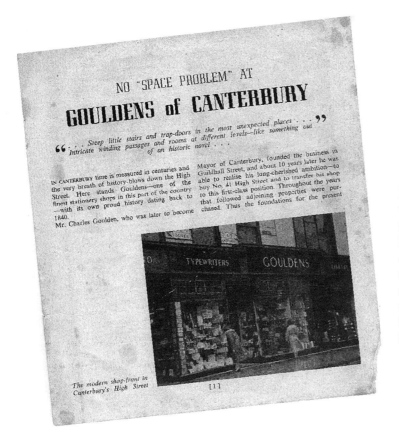

Booklet of happy memories

I am fortunate enough to own what I believe is one of the few surviving copies of a booklet written by Sophie Jacobs and published by Gouldens nearly 50 years ago. It describes the shop as customers would have found it at any time in the years immediately after the war.

The newspaper article in the image reads:

NO "SPACE PROBLEM" AT
GOULDENS of CANTERBURY

" . . . Steep little stairs and trap-doors in the most unexpected places . . . Intricate winding passages and rooms at different levels—like something out of an historic novel . . . "

IN CANTERBURY time is measured in centuries and the very breath of history blows down the High Street. Here stands Gouldens—one of the finest stationery shops in this part of the country —with its own proud history dating back to 1840.

Mr. Charles Goulden, who was later to become Mayor of Canterbury, founded the business in Guildhall Street, and about 10 years later he was able to realise his long-cherished ambition—to buy No. 41 High Street and to transfer his shop to this first-class position. Throughout the years that followed adjoining properties were purchased. Thus the foundations for the present

The modern shop-front in Canterbury's High Street

[1]

beautiful shop-front in the High Street and the large airy premises (several times rebuilt since) were firmly laid in the 19th century.

Mr. Charles Goulden was succeeded by his son Henry, who, incidentally, was a qualified chemist, and he in turn was succeeded by two of his sons, Gontran and Leslie. Mr. Gontran Goulden retired last year; Mr. Leslie is still actively engaged in running the piano shop which is now carried on as a separate concern at 36 High Street. The piano shop developed in rather an original way from the stationery shop. Henry Goulden, who was an enterprising man, bought a piano and engaged a young man to play it when a customer entered the shop, in order to encourage sales of sheet music and song sheets. When a customer wanted to buy the piano he sold it to him—on hire purchase, a rare thing in those days (about 1882). Soon another piano was sold and thus the music side of the business developed.

The full story of the development of the business of the enterprising and renowned Goulden family would fill many pages, but lack of space forces us to concentrate on the shop as it is today.

Taken over a year ago by Hatchards Ltd., Piccadilly, London, the shop continues to be run on the time-honoured lines and with the right degree of enterprise by Mr. S. T. Hart, a most able and competent manager. Mr. Hart has the quiet confidence of a man who knows and likes his job. With a lifetime's experience in the trade behind him, he joined Gouldens some 15 months ago

Top: Young customers take advantage of facilities in children's books section

Centre: A customer chooses paper serviettes; in foreground, wedding stationery display

Left: Display of Canterbury prints and view-cards

[2]

Top of page: two passers-by indulge in some window shopping on a rainy day in about 1950. Left: the children's book department; the counter where serviettes and wedding stationery could be purchased; and a display of Canterbury prints and postcards.

History in the High Street

The booklet traces the history of Gouldens back to 1840, when Charles Goulden, later Mayor of Canterbury, opened his first shop in Guildhall Street. In about 1850 he moved to the High Street, to premises which were extended several times as trade expanded.

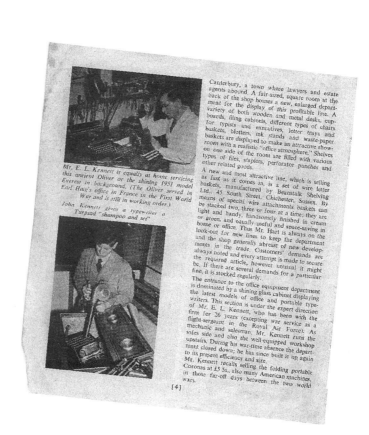

and continues to manage the business for the new owners.

The spacious, approximately L-shaped shop is strictly departmentalised and a model of effective interior display. Seventeen assistants are at the disposal of Mr. Hart and a senior assistant is in charge of each department, responsible for the appropriate window displays. These are changed roughly once a fortnight, but there is no regular routine. The large modern shop-front includes two islets and thus provides ample display space for the wide range of goods carried, including a representative typewriter display.

Though the stationery departments do a steady trade all the year round, part of the business is definitely seasonal in character. Every year at Easter-time tourists start to descend on Canterbury in a growing stream until their number rises to as many as 6-7,000 a day at the height of the summer. This enormous influx of people naturally brings a lot of trade to the town. Gouldens' large fancy goods department is kept busy, selling gifts and souvenirs, many of a religious nature, and a large selection of beautiful prints of old Canterbury is displayed for the visitors. Viewcards are ever-popular and, as a souvenir in the cheaper price ranges, viewcards which have been processed on to a special light, coloured frame, backs fitted for hanging or standing, are unusual, attractive and hard to beat for value at 2s. 6d. The same process has been used to good effect on children's and religious cards.

Office equipment is a line especially suitable in

Top: Display of artists' materials—Miss G. E. Iley sells a box of paints

Centre: Miss W. Uden, in foreground, serving in the private notepaper section of her department

Right: The commercial stationery department— a customer selects a telephone index

[3]

Top picture: artists' materials on Miss G.E. Iley's counter; Miss W. Uden serving private notepaper (one of my jobs in the 1930s); and a customer choosing a telephone index in the commercial stationery department. Right: Ted Kennett and his son John servicing and cleaning typewriters.

Mr. E. L. Kennett is equally at home servicing this ancient Oliver or the shining 1951 model Everest in background. (The Oliver served in Earl Haig's office in France in the First World War and is still in working order.)

John Kennett gives a typewriter a Turpsed "shampoo and set"

Canterbury, a town where lawyers and estate agents abound. A fair-sized, square room at the back of the shop houses a new, enlarged department for the display of this profitable line. A variety of both wooden and metal desks, cupboards, filing cabinets, different types of chairs for typists and executives, letter trays and baskets, blotters, ink stands and waste-paper baskets are displayed to make an attractive showroom with a realistic "office atmosphere." Shelves on one side of the room are filled with various types of files, staplers, perforator punches and other related goods.

A new and most attractive line, which is selling as fast as it comes in, is a set of wire letter baskets, manufactured by Beanstalk Shelving Ltd., 45 South Street, Chichester, Sussex. By means of special wire attachments baskets can be stacked two, three or four at a time; they are light and handy, handsomely finished in cream or green, and equally useful and space-saving in home or office. Thus Mr. Hart is always on the look-out for new lines to keep the department and the shop generally abreast of new developments in the trade. Customers' demands are always noted and every attempt is made to secure the required article, however unusual it might be. If there are several demands for a particular line, it is stocked regularly.

The entrance to the office equipment department is dominated by a shining glass cabinet displaying the latest models of office and portable typewriters. This section is under the expert direction of Mr. E. L. Kennett, who has been with the firm for 26 years (excepting war service as a flight-sergeant in the Royal Air Force). As mechanic and salesman, Mr. Kennett runs the well-equipped workshop upstairs. During his war-time absence the department closed down; he has since built it up again to its present efficiency and size. Mr. Kennett recalls selling the folding portable Coronas at £5 5s., also many American machines, in those far-off days between the two world wars.

[4]

Today Gouldens stock the Empire portable typewriter, the portable Oliver, Olympia and several Italian and Swiss models. Mr. Kennett is his firm's representative for the Typewriter Trades Federation. He runs a cleaning and overhauling service on contract for many Canterbury offices, including the city council offices and local hospitals. One of his eminent customers was the late Commander Gould, who wrote on the history of the typewriter and owned a fine collection of old typewriters which were serviced by Mr. Kennett.

Up in the workshop young John Kennett is learning the tricks of the trade from his craftsman father and is turning a useful hand to repairs. Machines are cleaned in a special machine with a pedal-release of a jet of Turpsad, and there is a big "blower"—looking like a hairdryer for a giant's daughter—to help clean the machines still further and get rid of eraser dust, etc. Other equipment for this up-to-date workshop includes a lathe for grinding platens, also drills and a grindstone-polisher, electrically operated. Mr. Kennett keeps a wide range of spare parts for most common and many uncommon makes of machines in neatly labelled drawers, and can undertake repairs of the most ancient and most modern machines.

Miss W. Uden is in charge of personal and table stationery—"all un-commercial items" she laughingly termed them—and her glass cases immediately to the left on entering the shop are filled with a wide variety of note papers, boxes, compendiums and pads. But her real love is the social stationery. The daintily displayed doyleys, baking cases and crimped paper cups cannot fail to induce Canterbury housewives to select a few additional items from so rich a selection. Paper serviettes are shown in a special rack which makes choice easy and saves excessive handling. Miss Uden, who hails from Whitstable, has worked for Gouldens for 11 years, with the exception of some war service in Chatham dockyards. She has been in charge of the department for just over two years.

[5]

A duplicator demonstration in the office equipment department. On left, Mr. S. T. Hart, manager, looks on. In background Mr. Kennett is showing a typewriter

Fancy goods and artists' materials, the latter particularly well-displayed, are in the care of Miss G. E. Iley. A "Wren" during the war, Miss Iley loves her job, which she has held for four-and-a-half years, and is particularly keen on the handling and selling of artists' materials. Encouraged by this and an artistic relative, she has recently taken up painting herself as a hobby and should find no lack of subjects in picturesque Canterbury or her nearby home in Sturry. Miss Iley also excels at window-dressing.

In addition to the office equipment department there is an old-established and well-stocked commercial stationery department at the top left hand corner of the long shop. Again the order and attractiveness of the display is strikingly combined with efficiency. There are rows of ledgers, files and account books on the shelves, while inks, rubber stamps, ink wells and other small incidental equipment are displayed on the counters. Mr. N. Goodban, the senior assistant in this department, was on a Twinlock sales-course when we visited the shop and we were, therefore, unable to meet him.

Turning round the bend of the "L" we move into the book department, which is in the care

The office equiment department, showing a duplicator being demonstrated while Mr T.S. Hart, the shop's manager, looks on and Ted Kennett inspects a typewriter which has been brought in for servicing.

of Mr. N. C. Allen and includes a much-frequented children's book section. Further along are greeting cards—the display changing according to the season—view cards and Canterbury and Kent prints.

From this department an open door leads into the piano shop—a friendly gesture and a concession to the people of Canterbury accustomed to go from one shop to another for many years. Mr. Hart led the way round the upper part of the premises and, with steep little stairs and trap doors in the most unexpected places, a guide was certainly necessary. The intricate winding passages and rooms at different levels—like something out of an historic novel—point to the great age of these houses. (The Royal Mint dating back to the 12th century was under No. 37 High Street; the basement is still visited by tourists.) The many rooms, large and small—now stock-rooms, offices, etc.—at one time housed the large Goulden family, and many of the children were born there. But here is the value of all this for Mr. Hart: he has no space problem (the first stationery shop we have seen that can boast this).

There is ample shelf space in the many stock rooms and, in addition, there is a book-binding department where small binding jobs are carried out. A special room has been comfortably fitted up as a rest room and is the much-appreciated sanctuary of the female staff.

The administrative work of the business is handled in a bright office with Miss B. Rose, chief clerk, in charge. There is a smaller office for the manager, but Mr. Hart laughingly admitted that he had no time during the day for sitting there and "usually spent his evenings in his office."

In common with the rest of Britain Canterbury awaits a record number of visitors for this Festival year. Its proximity to London, its great history and its beautiful cathedral would alone ensure this, but Canterbury has drawn up an ambitious Festival programme of its own. From 18th July to 10th August there will be concerts, plays, ballets, processions and flood-lighting. Gouldens of Canterbury are ready to welcome the tourists from all parts of the world.

SOPHIE JACOBS

10: Memories of home

The house where I was born. No. 7 St Dunstan's Street when it was my parents' shop in the 1930s and (right) as it is today. My bedroom was on the first floor, behind the window on the left of the picture.

EVEN though more than sixty years have passed since my parents and I left our shop in St Dunstan's I can remember every detail of the shop and our home. This is what I would have seen there at dusk on a winter's evening in 1921:

"I turn the door handle and enter the shop through the main door, glazed with frosted glass. The 'sweet window' is on my right, and the one on my left is full of cakes and buns. There are lots of mirrors all around the shop, so everything is duplicated by the reflections. Access to the windows is through a lift-up flap in the counter; on the counter there is a wooden till with a drawer. If it contains more than £2, Mum and Dad will have had a good day's trade.

"Also on the counter there is a glass chocolate case, and a collection box for Kent and Canterbury Hospital (then in Long-port). The box is tied to the counter by a piece of string — a necessary precaution because although burglaries are rare, the box was stolen one day.

A detail from my 'picture on the wall' (see page 5). It is 1921 and I am about to enter the side door to my parents' shop at No. 7 St Dunstan's Street. In the photograph on the opposite page I am standing in the same place 77 years later, in February 1998. The door is now the entrance to Coral's. In the 1920s the shop behind me, now the Capital Chinese Takeaway, was owned by Nash & Co., who sold military uniforms, breeches and ladies' costumes. The next shop along, on the corner of North Lane, was Sarah Welsh's sweet shop.

"Some brass scales, for weighing sweets and flour, also stand on the counter and all around the walls there are shelves holding sweets, big round glass bowls of biscuits (sold by the pound), glasses of all sizes for cold drinks, and an odd-looking iron ball full of string. I can't think why we need string — perhaps it is for tying-up boxes of chocolates and crackers at Christmas.

"Florrie's chair is in the corner. Florrie is Mum and Dad's assistant and she often sits there knitting while waiting for the next customer — a coat and hat for my doll, Betty Margaret, perhaps. Florrie is a good knitter; I am always running to her because I have 'dropped a stitch'. Behind her, on a hook, is a supply of bread-wrapping paper.

"Mum and Dad's office faces the shop door. There is a desk and a high stool in there, and ledgers of course, in which Alfred and Dad check-in the day's takings from their bread rounds.

"In the office there is a large, framed advertisement for Fry's Chocolate. It portrays five faces of a boy, each with a different expression — 'desperation,' 'pacification,' 'expectation', and so forth. Most of the space in the shop is taken by the tables and chairs for customers who call in for cups of tea and cakes.

"Walking through the shop, I come to our dining room. This contains a very big deal table, which seats eight people, a chiffonier in red wood, a sofa, two small tables, a corner cupboard where the best china is kept, my mother's work box — and our piano. This has a fretwork front lined with pink silk, and candles in two brass brackets; they are never lit, as Dad is very 'safety conscious.'

"Dad's chair is in one corner, his pipe rack to hand nearby. The fireplace has an overmantel with a big mirror, a lovely clock with such a pretty face, and two pairs of matching ornaments. On the hearth there is a redwood coal box and a brass shovel. All our

floors are covered with linoleum and there are no carpets — just a rug here and there.

"On the dining room wall are large photos of my brother and me (I still have them). Harry has been photographed against a very dark background and what looks like a tree. It looks as if he is sitting in a cemetery! In my photo I am sitting on a table, holding a doll which has had both it eyes pushed in! I insisted on holding it.

"Over the sofa there is a very big picture of Folkestone seafront, showing the pier and a toll gate which, I think, was in Lower Sandgate Road. A picture called 'The Return of the Life Boat' hangs above the piano.

"Aspidistras are very popular, but I don't like them because they have no flowers. We have one in the window facing the back yard, and a cactus which never seems to bloom.

"On Friday nights we have a bath, which is put in front of the fire and filled with hot water brought in buckets. I'll never forget that smell of Pear's soap. When I was younger and Mum washed my hair I screamed all the time. It was then put into rag curlers.

"Compared with the other rooms our kitchen is very small and, as I mentioned before, we do not have a cooker, just a gas ring on which stands our large kettle for making tea for the customers in the shop. The kitchen chair is used for many things — not just to sit on. It is pretty old yet never wears out. Mum scrubs it and it is always spotlessly clean.

"Our pantry is a big cupboard. Our kitchen sink is not very deep, so Mum washes all our clothes in a big enamel bowl.

"We have no room for a washing line in the back yard — the bread barrows and trade bicycles take up nearly all the space — so we dry the washing in a loft, which is reached by a ladder.

"My bedroom is on the first floor, facing St Dunstan's Street. It contains a bed, a chest of drawers and a dressing table — and cold lino on the floor! In one corner there is a low table (actually I think it is a commode!) covered with a pretty cloth. On the table stands my collection of photographs of Kent cricketers — Leslie Ames, W.A. Ashdown, A.P.F. Chapman, Tich Freeman, Harold Hardinge, Frank Woolley and others.

"It is very much in fashion to hang pictures from a picture rail. All our pictures tell a story. One of mine is called 'The Guardian Angel' and shows a little girl walking by a ditch, with some flowers she has gathered. The Angel is walking at her side with one hand on her shoulder. Another of my pictures depicts Queen Victoria's death and shows her sitting on her throne, surrounded by angels!

"I also have a big chest of linen in my room, and a fireplace. I cannot remember ever having a fire but in times of illness, such as when I had scarlet fever, I had a Valor oil lamp, which threw lovely, mysterious, patterns on the ceiling when it was getting dark.

☐ ☐ ☐

"Looking out of my window I can see Mr Grant standing at the door of Fletcher's, the butchers, and Nellie Penny serving in the fish shop. Mr Skelton is standing at the door of 'The Gun' Dining Rooms and Dad is carrying a tray of cakes or bread across the road to him.

"I was born in Mum and Dad's bedroom, which is also on the first floor. It has two windows overlooking the street. There is a marble-topped washstand on which stands a big china jug and basin. We do not have a bathroom, so hot water has to be carried upstairs to our rooms. There are also two chamber pots, decorated with flowers!

"Mum and Dad's bedroom furniture consists of a chest of drawers, a dressing table, a cupboard (but no wardrobe) and a table by the window sporting the inevitable aspidistra. Their bed is a brass affair, with big highly polished knobs. There are several ornaments in the room — one of them is made of celluloid (I wish I had saved it, as it is probably now quite rare). A glass stick with a crook hangs on the wall. I don't know what its purpose is; it may have been used at one time to light a lamp by pulling down the chain that regulated the gas.

"My brother Harry's bedroom is also on the first floor. It is a rather dark room, with a window looking on to the back yard. The room has a very dark corner and I always find it a bit 'creepy.'

"There are two flights of stairs in the house, and a landing on the first floor. On the left of the stairs there are two very large and very old oil paintings in gilt frames. It is almost impossible to see any details but if I look very closely I can just make out some trees, a

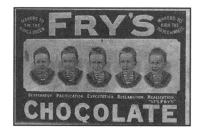

The advertisement in Dad's office for Fry's Chocolate.

Housework was hard work when we lived at No. 7 St Dunstan's Street, and 'Spring cleaning' was an annual upheaval.

St Dunstan's, more than 60 years ago and in 1998. In the top picture my father and the other shopkeepers have hung up their window blinds, which tells us that it is either a Thursday (early closing day) or a Sunday – probably early afternoon. No doubt the owners of the motor car and the motor cycle and side car are still enjoying their lunch in the *Falstaff*. In the distance, just past the man with the barrow, we see the arcaded frontage to G.W. Wilkinson's boot and shoe shop on the corner of Station Road West. On the opposite corner is a water fountain and Teal's corn and fruit shop. On the left of the picture an Army officer and his girlfriend walk arm in arm, while he pushes her bicycle. I like to think that she cycled to meet him at the bus station in St Peter's Place and is taking him home to meet her parents! The 1998 view shows that most of the buildings at this end of St Dunstan's have survived, the only modern properties being those near Kirby's Lane and Station Road West, built to replace ones that were bombed during the last war.

St. Dunstan's Street, Canterbury.

building (probably a house) and one or two people. I think the paintings came with the business when Dad bought it in 1907.

"On the landing there is a long sideboard with drawers, on top of which are books and yet more ornaments, and a glass dome-shaped case on a corner shelf. Under the dome there are flowers and stuffed, coloured birds — reminders of the Victorian era.

"On the top floor there are two rooms. One is a bedroom for visitors, the other contains a dressing table. In the afternoon Florrie changes there into her afternoon dress and white pinafore or apron, before serving teas. Florrie has a lovely head of hair, very black and shiny, reaching to her waist. I like to brush it before she rolls it up into a 'bun'.

"There is a pole in the centre of 'Florrie's room,' reaching from floor to ceiling. It is a bit of a mystery as it is too slender to support the ceiling, but it was obviously put there for a purpose. We use the room as a playroom when my cousins Doris and Harold come to stay — 'Let's go Up Top,' we say.

"The bakehouse is at the back of the building and has a stone floor, drawers containing fruit for the cakes, great tubs of fat, two troughs of flour to make the bread, large metal mixing bowls, and some scales. The baking oven is heated by a coal furnace, and

Dad uses a baker's long-handled shovel to put the loaves in and out; it's called a 'peel' and is rather like a child's sand spade, though much larger. For cleaning the oven he has another special bakehouse implement, called a 'scuffle.' After he has used it he will walk across St Dunstan's Street to the river bank in Westgate Grove, and wash it from the foot of the steps that lead down to the water's edge.

"When everyone is busy working our cat sits watching the mouse hole and makes a grab when one ventures too close. Black beetles infest the bakehouse but there are other pests too — wasps in the summer, and lots of flies. We have no fly sprays, only sticky fly papers baited with sugar hanging from the ceiling.

☐ ☐ ☐

"Mum often works in the bakehouse with Dad, making ginger nuts and sponge cakes. She makes quite a lot of cakes, and Dad and Alfred make all the bread. If anyone in the bakehouse wants to talk to someone in the shop, or vice-versa, they do so via a long rubber tube, a kind of 'inter-com.' To attract attention you blow into the tube and this sounds a whistle. You then speak into the tube and hold it to your ear for the reply!

"We dust every room each day, and brush the stairs. House-work is hard work! 'Spring cleaning' is an annual upheaval. We start the day by 'having the sweep,' in the person of Mr Twyman, who lives in Northgate. He is always asked to come early in the morning, so the night before he turns up we remove everything from the dining room or cover it with sheets. We take the pictures down and clean them, polish the furniture, wash the curtains, floors and linoleum, and beat the daylights out of the rugs.

"Eventually everything will be spick and span — until next year, when we will do it all over again!"

☐ ☐ ☐

I walked along St Dunstan's the other day and stood opposite my old home, which is now a betting office. The lower facade has changed; there is no longer a central front door, only the side door. I looked up at the first floor, to the room with two windows which was my parents' bedroom.

My brother Harry and I were born in this room. The room on the left, adjoining the *Falstaff*, was my bedroom. Harry's bedroom was at the back of the house, overlooking the yard.

On the second floor I saw that the windows of the two 'spare rooms' — one was a storeroom and playroom, the other was a spare bedroom — are also still as I remember them. I sat for hours with my friends at the window on the right, watching the world go by and taking car numbers.

I noticed the cellar grating in the pavement outside the shop, and imagined how damp and dark it must be down there. The cellar had an earth floor. I wondered how long it has been since anyone ventured down the steps.

The trap door above the cellar is probably now under the floor of the betting shop. Perhaps it will be many years before the cellar sees the light of day again.

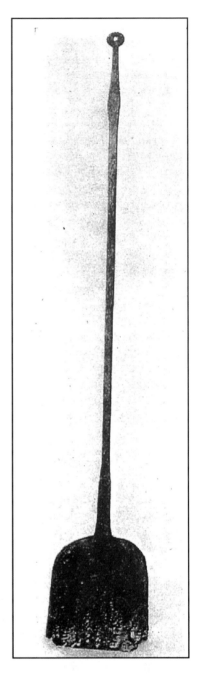

A baker's oven 'peel.'

11: Life in St Lawrence

Below: children and their parents from the St Lawrence Road and Barton Estate areas in May 1945, at their VE Day party in a field beside New Dover Road.

AFTER living in St Dunstan's, one of Canterbury's oldest districts, for the first 23 years of my life, I was destined to move to the opposite end of the city, to one of its newer suburbs — St Lawrence — and I have now lived here for more than 60 years.

The St Lawrence district is on the Old Dover Road, between Ethelbert Road and Nackington Road, and is not without its own history. In the Middle Ages there was a hospital here, and no doubt a church or chapel: they would have been among the first and last buildings travellers passed as they left or approached Canterbury via Watling Street, of which the Old Dover Road is part.

The hospital was founded in 1137 for lepers from St Augustine's Abbey and named after Laurentius, principal sextus to the Bishop of Rome. I pass a relic of the building every time I walk home from the town — it is a short length of stone and brick wall near the corner of St Lawrence Forstal.

There was once a gruesome carving in the wall, depicting the saint being tortured by fire on a gridiron. Forty years ago you could still see most of the gory details but they are now too eroded to be recognisable to anyone who does not know the story.

St Lawrence is famous for its cricket ground, the headquarters of Kent County Cricket Club. Among the many fine houses hereabouts are some that date back to Victorian times, showing

St Lawrence Cottage, awaiting new owners having been the Ellen family's home for nearly 60 years. The single storey extension was the Ellens' greengrocer's shop and was originally a laundry.

that this has been a popular residential area for more than a hundred years.

Anyone who has lived in the area for 40 years or more remembers the St Lawrence Steam Laundry in St Lawrence Forstal, and its hooter which was sounded at five minutes to eight every morning to remind the workers that it was nearly time to 'clock in,' and a few minutes before the beginning and end of the lunch hour.

When we decided to get married, Ted and I chose a house in St Lawrence Road, between Old Dover Road and New Dover Road. Our wedding was at St Martin's Church, Herne, on June 3, 1937 — the day Edward VIII and Wallis Simpson were married.

It was a lovely day. My bridesmaids were Norah Child, my future sister-in-law, and my cousin Doris. Our reception was in Herne Village Hall, with around 30 guests, and I still have the receipt from the baker in Herne who did the catering.

We went to a boarding house at Shanklin, on the Isle of Wight, for our honeymoon. It was nearly a disaster. I had forgotten to confirm our reservation and the landlady wasn't expecting us. Luckily she had a vacant room.

At the cottage gate. 'Look at my new trousers!' is what Chris Tritton appears to be saying to Allan Taylor in this picture of a group of St Lawrence Road children in 1950. Also in the photo are (from the left) Susan and Diana Ellen from St Lawrence Cottage and John Taylor. The Taylors lived at No. 11 St Lawrence Road.

Old Dover Road from St Lawrence Cricket Ground on Boxing Day, 1956, and (below) in April 1998. Town houses have replaced most of the old cottages but the *Bat & Ball* pub is still there to welcome its regulars and cricket followers.

All that remains of the effigy in Old Dover Road depicting St Lawrence's ordeal on the gridiron. His torturer can just be made out on the right, holding his flesh-hook!

Ted worked for Robert Brett & Sons, and in the course of his work he visited various builders. One of them was Stroud & Roberts of Whitstable, who were building eight three-bedroom, semi-detached houses on land that had been part of a small-holding run by William Ellen. There were no other houses in the road, except the four Vidgen-Wilson Almshouses behind our 'local,' the *Bat & Ball* pub, on the corner of Old Dover Road.

We chose plot No. 8, in the centre of the row. The price of the house was £760. Ted was earning £4.10s.0d. a week and he put by £4.2s.10d. a month for the mortgage. It took us 25 years to repay it. We named our home Rylestone, after Rylestone Gardens, Shanklin, which we often visited during our honeymoon.

The houses are mock-Tudor in style, quite attractive and well built, and had what we called 'character'. The front rooms had leaded light windows but when my mother saw them she warned me that they would be difficult to clean. So we told the builders to replace them with plain glazing! They also had to replace the leaded lights in the front rooms of No. 7, otherwise the two 'semis' would not have looked like a pair! That made Nos 7 and 8 different in one small detail to the other houses in the road.

St Lawrence Road on Boxing Day, 1956 and (below) more than 41 years later, in April 1998, showing the mock-Tudor houses built in 1937 and, in the distance, the stables which today are known as The Coach House. The telephone pole was in our front garden and we received a wayleave payment of 7s 6d a year from the GPO. Most of the original horse-chestnut trees growing beside the road became diseased in the 1980s and were felled, but their replacements are thriving. Modern lamp posts have taken the place of the ornate, swan-necked ones erected in the 1930s and 'wheelie bins' instead of dustbins are taken to the pavement for the weekly refuse collection.

Having been part of Mr Ellen's smallholding our back garden had two apple trees, a plum tree and a rhubarb patch. Over the years, while gardening, we found hundreds of clay pipe stems but only one bowl. They were probably 17th century.

When Ted built a rockery in our front garden he found some coloured paving, probably mosaic. I wonder if it came from the old leper hospital?

Our immediate neighbours were Mr and Mrs David Gray at No. 10 – he was the manager of Timothy Whites & Taylors, the chemists in The Parade; and Mr and Mrs Bowley at No. 7 – he was the head of the General Post Office in Canterbury. Mr and Mrs Fowler lived at No. 5 (the first new house in the row) and the Redferns were at No. 6. Mr Hamilton, who ran a wine and spirit business, and Mrs Hamilton were at No. 11, Austen ('Mick') Phillips (a baker) and his family lived at No. 12, and the end house was the home of the Gibbs family.

The smallholding I mentioned belonged to St Lawrence Cottage, which became No. 9 St Lawrence Road when the new houses were built in 1937. The cottage lays back from the road, almost out of sight, and people who don't know it is there wonder

In the 1940s and 1950s children from the St Lawrence area attended Wincheap County Primary School, a mile away. Few parents had cars, nor was there a school bus, so most of the pupils walked to school and back in all weathers. Those who did so in the years immediately after the war made their through orchards and hop-gardens that were rapidly being replaced by the bricks and mortar of the Oxford Road and Zealand Road housing estates. The picture below shows a class of 38 children and their teacher. My son Chris is sitting at the right hand end of the second row from the front. Other pupils identified are: Peter Cole (sixth from left, back row), Kenneth Clitheroe (eighth from left, back row), Sandra Barling (second from left, third row from front), Rose May (third from left, second row from front), Brian Carter (sixth from left, front row) and Peter Floyd (at the right hand end of the front row).

why the numbers of the houses fronting St Lawrence Road 'jump' from 8 to 10.

Another curiosity is that there is no No. 13. The next house on from No. 12 is No. 14.

No. 9 is a charming Victorian cottage and looks just like a doll's house. It is built of mellow red bricks and tiles, and has a centre porch at its front door, with two windows on either side of the door and three windows on the first floor.

The cottage is surrounded by fruit trees and fruit bushes — a small orchard, in fact — and there is also a fig tree, rose bushes, and all kinds of cottage garden flowers.

No one seems to know all that much about the cottage's history except that it dates from the nineteenth century, and that the single storey extension on its south side was once a laundry.

I remember that for some years there was an old-fashioned copper in there, with a fire underneath to boil the washing water; the little hatch in the wall that let the steam out is still there.

In the 1920s St Lawrence Cottage was the home of the Tucker sisters but from the time we lived at No. 8 until 1995 the tenants were the Ellens. 'Old Mr Ellen,' his son Ernest and daughter Ada ran a shop from what used to be the laundry.

They sold their own produce — vegetables, fruit in season and honey from their bees.

'Ern' did his deliveries on his bicycle and Ada served the customers who came from all around, walking to the shop down the side road between our house and No. 10, or along a path that branched off the Old Dover Road.

It was a very popular little shop, and so convenient to be able to pop down and buy freshly picked beans, and potatoes that had been dug up that very morning.

Everyone liked Ada. When the cherries were ripening on their trees she would sit out in the early morning, scaring the birds off by banging a tin.

Every Cricket Week, in the Thirties, 'Ern' put up a notice up saying that bicycles could be left at the cottage for 6d while their owners enjoyed a 'day at the cricket.' Sadly 'Ern' died in 1995. His

wife Doris has moved from the cottage to another part of Canterbury but I see her and her daughters Sue and Diana quite often.

□ □ □

At one time there was a row of picturesque cottages just round the corner from us in Old Dover Road. They extended from No. 135, where Mr and Mrs Coombs lived, to the *Bat & Ball* pub. My mother lived in one of them (No. 151) when she was in her late 80s, before moving to one of the Vidgen-Wilson Almshouses and, in the last years of her life, to our house.

No. 151 was typical of the cottages and had a large front room, a kitchen, two bedrooms, an attic, a cellar – and a lavatory at the bottom of the garden! The stairs to the bedrooms were steep and dark and, from the front bedroom, there was a fine view of the cricket ground.

One day my son Chris and some of his friends managed to get into the cellar of Mrs Skippen's cottage next door, where they were discovered enjoying on of their 'feasts.' Among Mum's other neighbours were the Eldridge family at No. 145; Jim Eldridge worked at the cricket ground.

Mum's cottage and I think several of the others belonged to George Coombs, who lived with his wife and son John at No. 135 ((Kingdom Cottage) at the end of the row. The Coombs' cottage was larger than the others and Mr Coombs added many attractive features, using 'odds and ends' such as pieces of stained glass. Their little 'old world' garden was always 'a picture.'

The cottages would be treasured today but sadly most of them were demolished in the 1960s to make way for a row of 'town houses.' The sites of two of the cottages are now occupied by the *Bat and Ball's* extension and car park.

□ □ □

Join me for a walk down New Dover Road in 1937.

From my home in St Lawrence Road I turn left at my gate, cross the side road to St Lawrence Cottage, and pass No. 10 (Mr and Mrs Gray), No. 11 (Mr and Mrs Hamilton), No. 12 (Mr and Mrs Philips), and No. 14 (Mr and Mrs Gibbs). Next come some stables belonging to some people living in the New Dover Road. Mr and Mrs Barber live on the corner of St Lawrence Road — so we call it 'Barbers' Corner'.

As I walk towards the town, nearly all the houses I pass are private residences. Soon one of them will become the King's School Boarding House, for masters and scholars, and every day I will meet the boys in their smart uniform and straw 'boaters,' walking back from school for their meals.

Some of the boaters will have been 'bashed in' on purpose; perhaps someone objected to them!

Further down, behind some very old tall trees, is a bungalow called The Grove. This is the home of Sandra Tchitchérin, a member of a Russian family that fled to England during the Revolution.

Before the railway bridge I pass the Abbots Barton Hotel and recall that before it became a hotel it was the home of Mr Francis

The *Bat & Ball* pub, popular with cricket fans and local residents since the turn of the century and especially busy during the war when soldiers were billeted in St Lawrence Villas. In those days the pub was run by Henry and Betty DeCosta.

At a birthday party in St Lawrence Road in 1944. Sally Phillips from No. 12 is third from the left in the middle row. The two children on the left in the front row are Diana Ellen and Paul Tritton. Roberta Mallett from No. 7 is at the other end of the row. Rosemary Vining from New Dover Road is standing at the back. The other children were friends from St Bede's School, Old Dover Road. Bottom of opposite page: Ted and me at our new home in 1937.

The entrance to the Vidgen-Wilson Almshouses, founded by Mary Elizabeth Wilson in 1925.

The view from our front door in July 1962, showing one of St Lawrence Road's original ornate 1930s street lamps. They were adorned with 'swan necks' and decorative mouldings. We bought this one when the lamps were replaced in the 1970s.

Bennett-Goldney, Mayor of Canterbury. Just over the railway bridge is Drayton House, once occupied by another Mayor of Canterbury, Catherine Williamson. A little further down I pass 'Maxwelton' (No. 46), the home of Miss Hughes D'Aeth, 'Belswains' (No. 47), the home of Mr George Browning, JP, and the site of Ersham House, on which Telephone House will soon take shape. There is a 'pets' cemetery' in the front garden of 'Belswains.' At the end of New Dover Road, on the corner of Upper Chantry Lane, are the new and very modern premises of Maltby's Motor Works and Garage.

□ □ □

I was at home in St Lawrence Road when at midday on September 3, 1939 we had our first air raid warning. It was a Sunday, but Ted had gone to work at Bretts' office at No. 16 St George's Place because the firm was preparing for war.

When the siren went off I took my 13-month-old son Paul along to No. 6, to join all our other neighbours. I don't quite know why we went there – perhaps we felt safer, not knowing what to expect. We all sat in their dining room, almost surrounded by windows! Anyhow it was a false alarm, and the 'all clear' soon sounded.

In 1940, women and children were evacuated from Canterbury and Paul and I went to Botley, near Oxford. We were billeted with some friendly people and had a room with a coal fire, where I could heat some soup and make hot drinks.

I can't remember where we had our lunches but I think communal meals were served somewhere.

I was billeted near a friend from Canterbury, Kit Field, who was with her little girl, Daphne, who was the same age as Paul.

After a week or two we all returned to Canterbury, as we were so homesick!

The day before we arrived there was an air raid while Ted was cleaning the kitchen floor. He dived into the cupboard under the stairs, which was considered to be the safest place in the house; it became our refuge on several nights, and we sat there sipping hot drinks.

Later, Ted and a neighbour built an Anderson shelter in our back garden. There was room for six adults and Paul in his wicker cot. We spent the night of the Canterbury Blitz — June 1/2, 1942 — down there. When we came out next morning after the 'all clear' had sounded, the first thing I noticed was that, despite all the mayhem, a little flower garden that Paul and his friend Sally Phillips had made the previous afternoon around the base of one of our apple trees was completely undisturbed.

I was more relieved to see that all the houses in the road were still standing; however, to this day the side windows in my lounge and dining room show the effect of the bomb blasts. They bulge outwards. Bretts' offices, only half a mile away, were destroyed.

My brother Harry was stationed with an AA Battery on St Thomas's Hill and saw Canterbury burning. The next day I walked through the smouldering ruins with Paul in his pushchair and caught a bus to Herne, to stay with my parents for a few days.

Later we had a daylight raid. I was walking home up New Dover Road after shopping in the town when I saw some low-flying aeroplanes coming from the Dover direction. Not until they were overhead did I realise they were German planes! I could see the pilots, and the swastikas painted on the wings.

I took shelter in the ARP Warden's post in the stable yard, next door to No. 14 St Lawrence Road. When I got home I found that Ted, Paul and Mrs Gray had dived into our Anderson shelter.

A number of people were killed during this raid and Burgate Street was damaged.

Mr and Mrs Hamilton had a super underground shelter, with gas-tight doors and a toilet! I took refuge there with Paul during one alert. The shelter is still there.

We had a barrage balloon unit in the New Dover Road. When the 'doodle bugs' started coming over Mr Gray went along to ask the men in charge what they were but they wouldn't tell him!

We found out soon enough!

☐ ☐ ☐

At our home in St Lawrence Road, Ted and I brought up our two sons. Edward Paul was born on August 8, 1938, at Canterbury Maternity Hostel in Dane John Gardens. Christopher Charles was born there on January 18, 1947.

Paul married Patricia Sackett in 1959. They have two children: Carole, born in 1961 and Stephen, born in 1963.

Chris married Janet Edney on March 9, 1968, and they have two sons: Neil, born in 1969 and Robert, born in 1972.

In 1980 Chris married Linda Glover. Their children are Genette, born in 1981 and Paul born in 1983.

Carole married Andrew Vidler in 1980. They have two sons, Mark, born in 1984 and Michael born in 1986.

Stephen married Belinda Wells in 1987 and they have a son, Thomas James, born in 1993.

There were no council schools in the St Lawrence area so both my sons went to Wincheap County Primary School, off Hollow Lane. It was quite a long way from where we lived – a mile, I would say – and of course like most children in those days, they had to walk it! In those days their route took them along footpaths between orchards and hop-gardens, which soon disappeared to make way for the housing estates in Oxford Road and Zealand Road.

☐ ☐ ☐

In 1986, 49 years after we moved to St Lawrence Road, I noted these changes:

"Most of the big houses in New Dover Road are now flats or offices and the one that was the King's School Boarding House has been converted into flats. Boys from 'King's' are no longer seen.

"Drayton House was damaged in the Second World War and later demolished; a block of flats now stands on the site. Miss Tchitchérin's bungalow is still in good condition. Ted and I, and Phylis Brown (Mr and Mrs Gibbs' daughter) at No. 14 are St Lawrence Road's only original residents.

"Some of the horse chestnut trees that line the road have had to be felled, but new young ones were planted."

Making mischief in St Lawrence Road in the 1940s: Andrea Owen from No. 11, John Mayes (whose grandmother, Mrs Gray, lived at No. 10) and Paul Tritton. The fire was probably lit by Brian Phillips from No. 12, who was always having bonfires.

Graham Blissett (left), whose father worked at St Lawrence Cricket Ground, and Chris Tritton in concert in our back garden, watched by Susan Ellen (left) and other friends.

St Lawrence Cricket Ground, Boxing Day, 1956. In the 1950s the seats around the boundary were uncomfortable wooden benches and, between cricket seasons, sheep grazed in the rough grass beyond the boundary – hence the fence in front of the seats and the hurdle in front of the old scorebox, which was replaced in 1998.

12: Canterbury Cathedral

Below: the Precincts of Canterbury Cathedral, where I have spent many happy hours.

IN my final chapter I would like to include some of my memories of Canterbury Cathedral, which span nearly nine decades. First, join me for a walk in the Cloisters

I enter Christ Church Gate and walk across The Precincts into the Cloisters. All around the walls, if I look hard enough, I see names, initials and carvings done by novice monks. Quite often a curious picture is encountered — an outline of a tower, with a flag on top. What is it? A representation of the cathedral? A mason's mark? The idle scratchings of novice monks? I have been asking this question for many years but no one seems certain.

One of the 'welcomers' said he understood that they *are* masons' marks, carved to show where they stopped work each day, but I am still not sure. They are both too detailed and too crudely carved for me to be convinced by this explanation.

I once saw exactly the same picture carved behind a door in a cottage near Hoath parish church.

In the Cloisters I also find carvings of the soles of feet, with dates. I imagine these were the work of young novice monks, amusing themselves between the lessons which they attended in the cloisters.

I also find round holes carved in the stone benches; was this where they played marbles?

At the end of the North Alley, by a very old door, there is a round aperture, where a monk or pilgrim could receive re-

freshment, maybe a glass of ale. He would take it and his identity would not be revealed! The doorway once led to the cellarium, where the monks stored their wine and provisions.

Opposite the Archdeacon's garden gate I come across another relic of monastic life – a bay where the monks washed. Nearby there is the very interesting water tower, once fed by a conduit from springs to the north-east of Canterbury.

Look closely and you will see names carved on the tower in the 17th century. One of them, in lovely Old English script, is MARY.

I often walk around the Cloisters and always find something I have not seen before.

□ □ □

I wrote the following impressions after a visit on January 19, 1978 — a cold, very dark, day.

"When one enters the cathedral on such a day as this, it is quiet and still. The atmosphere is indescribable — soft lighting, and a feeling of peace. There are no tourists, just one or two local people sitting in the nave after shopping, and one or two vergers and workmen going about their duties.

"I used to talk to the vergers - one was Sydney Fridd; another was John Durbin. Sadly, they have both passed away.

"The nave and choir had been full to capacity for the Christmas Eve service. When all the seats were taken people were allowed to sit on the nave steps.

"After a while I go down into the crypt, where there is so much to see if one really takes enough trouble. The Chapel of Our Lady Undercroft is one of the oldest parts. I pass the spot where Thomas Becket was entombed before being moved above to Trinity Chapel, beyond the High Altar.

"I look up at the vaults and see the rings from which lamps once hung, surrounded by circles of paintings. They are very worn but I can see the crown of thorns around one of them.

"I take a look at the 'ghost of Becket' on one of the pillars. I read somewhere that this is a mark left by the coal that at one time was stored in the east end of the crypt.

"Anyhow, it is nice to imagine it is Becket's ghost!

"There is another 'ghost' on a wall outside,. As you walk to the Dark Entry from the Cloisters you will notice, on your left, what appears to be a woman with a broom. It is said to be ghost of Nellie Cook, a servant girl who came to a bad end."

□ □ □

I still visit the cathedral nearly every day, after I have been shopping, and I constantly discover fresh things to look at. I am a member of the 'Friends of Canterbury Cathedral' and I enjoy taking part in their activities.

The Christmas Crib was a delight last year, and this year, I believe for the first time, there was an Easter garden, with palm trees and an empty tomb.

And I still peer at the walls and columns for ancient drawings!

The Cloisters in the early 1930s, when the Garth resembled a country churchyard. The gravestones were removed many years ago.

Two examples in the Cloisters of the curious carvings of a tower and flag that adorn some of the cathedral's walls and columns.

Index

Figures in bold type refer to picture captions

The parish of St Dunstan's and the Westgate area of Canterbury viewed from the top of Canterbury Cathedral's 235 ft high Bell Harry Tower on May 30, 1998. St Dunstan's Street runs diagonally across the picture, from the Westgate Towers (foreground, left) to St Dunstan's Church. Landmarks to the left of the church include the terraced houses in London Road and the chapel in Canterbury Cemetery, while on the right Whitstable Road starts to ascend St Thomas' Hill. Among the buildings in the foreground are the roof of the Marlowe Theatre and, facing the camera, the former City Police Station in Pound Lane.

To be published in 1999 in aid of local charities ...

'A Canterbury Tale'
Memories of a wartime movie
by Paul Tritton

FILMED on location in and around Canterbury and at Denham Studios in 1943 and 1944, *A Canterbury Tale* has been admired for many years for its unforgettable images of the gentle pace of life in Canterbury's countryside more than 50 years ago, and for its dramatic and moving final scenes set in Canterbury Cathedral and amidst the bombsites that scarred the city after the Blitz of June 1942.

• • •

Film director and producer Michael Powell, born at Bekesbourne and educated at King's School, Canterbury, returned to the city and landscapes he loved in his boyhood, to create a timeless story of pilgrimage and penance inspired by Chaucer's *Canterbury Tales.*

A Canterbury Tale had its world premiere at Canterbury's Friars Cinema (now the Marlowe Theatre) in May 1944, before an audience that included the film's director and stars, and many local people who appeared in the film as extras, befriended the cast and production unit, or witnessed scenes being filmed in Canterbury and at Chilham, Fordwich, Littlebourne, Selling, Shottenden, Wickhambreaux and Wingham.

• • •

While writing his book about *A Canterbury Tale,* Paul Tritton has collected many location and studio 'stills,' taken photographs of the locations as they appear today, interviewed the surviving members of the cast – Sheila Sim (Lady Attenbor-

ough), John Sweet, Len Smith and David Todd – and production team, and talked to many local people who have personal memories of wartime Canterbury and the film unit's visits to the city.

• • •

For more details and a priority order form, send a stamped self-addressed envelope to Paul Tritton, 2 Salts Avenue, Loose, Maidstone, Kent ME15 0AY, England.

You will receive details one month before publication date. If enquiring from outside the UK please send two International Reply Coupons.